the *Walk* *of* *Shame*

the Walk of Shame

a survival guide

ROBIN ANDERTON
AND JAY DESARIO

Roadside Amusements
a member of Penguin Group (USA) Inc.
New York

ROADSIDE AMUSEMENTS
an imprint of
CHAMBERLAIN BROS.
Published by the Penguin Group
Penguin Group (USA) Inc., 375 Hudson Street, New York, New York 10014, USA
Penguin Group (Canada), 90 Eglinton Avenue East, Suite 700, Toronto, Ontario
M4P 2Y3, Canada (a division of Pearson Penguin Canada Inc.)
Penguin Books Ltd, 80 Strand, London WC2R 0RL, England
Penguin Ireland, 25 St Stephen's Green, Dublin 2, Ireland (a division of Penguin
Books Ltd)
Penguin Group (Australia), 250 Camberwell Road, Camberwell, Victoria 3124,
Australia (a division of Pearson Australia Group Pty Ltd)
Penguin Books India Pvt Ltd, 11 Community Centre, Panchsheel Park, New
Delhi–110 017, India
Penguin Group (NZ), Cnr Airborne and Rosedale Roads, Albany, Auckland 1310,
New Zealand (a division of Pearson New Zealand Ltd)
Penguin Books (South Africa) (Pty) Ltd, 24 Sturdee Avenue, Rosebank,
Johannesburg 2196, South Africa

Penguin Books Ltd, Registered Offices: 80 Strand, London WC2R 0RL, England

LIBRARY OF CONGRESS CATALOGING-IN-PUBLICATION DATA
Anderton, Robin.
  The walk of shame / by Robin Anderton and Jay Desario.
    p. cm.
  ISBN 1-59609-047-2
  1. Young adults—Sexual behavior. 2. Young adults—Sexual behavior—Humor.
  3. College students—Sexual behavior—Humor. 4. Promiscuity. 5. Alcohol and
  sex. I. Desario, Jay. II. Title.
  HQ27.A655 2005   2005041329
  306.7'084'2—dc22

Printed in the United States of America
10 9 8 7 6 5 4 3 2 1

Book design and illustrations by Melissa Gerber

Contents

What Is the Walk of Shame?

This is a question that—as recognized experts on the topic—we're asked fairly often, usually by twelve-year-olds. Are you twelve years old? If you're twelve years old, sweetie, you really shouldn't be reading this book: it contains lots of dirty words, and a variety of jokes about anal sex. If you don't know what "anal sex" means, either, you should go ask your mother. In a few years you'll go to high school, and a bunch of guys from the wrestling team will try to convince you that all the *cool* girls do it.

Seriously, go away, ask her.

Now, if you're still reading, you're hopefully not twelve years old. In fact, according to our editor, we're legally obligated to hope you're at least eighteen, and—long story—

in no way associated with the estate of the late Aristotle Onassis. Which brings us to our next question: are you kidding? You seriously don't know what the Walk of Shame is? Surely you've wondered what that girl was doing out at eight in the morning in stiletto heels and a halter top?

Here's how to answer that question for yourself. First, go home and change into your tightest jeans. Keep in mind the sole sensible thing Jay's grandmother ever said: "Bras are for nuns." Now go out and drink something stiffer than an amaretto sour, for Christ's sake. Play with your hair a little. Bend over and pick stuff up. Bend from the waist, not the knees. When a song you enjoy comes on, walk over to the nearest man, fall over on top of him, and say, "Ohmygod, I like totally *love* this song"—this is the kind of intriguing, intelligent conversation that lets men know you're a woman to be treasured. Then take it to the next level of sophistication: go "whoo!" and rub your boobs against him.

Are you back? With any luck, you've just experienced the Walk of Shame, up close and in person. Let us guess: you woke up all groggy in some strange apartment or dorm room. One that turned out to be located on the one magical block that ensured you had to walk past every single person you've

ever known on your stumbling, groaning, skanky-looking
way back home. Your hair looks like the habitat for some rare
and ferocious rodent, and your breath smells about like it
should when your tongue's gone off, soaked itself in tequila,
and wound up passing out in someone *else's* mouth. With any
luck, you're hungover, slobbered on, über-skeezy, and—one
would hope—satisfied.

Welcome, friends, to the Walk of Shame. If this has never
happened to you before, you need to buy some shorter skirts.

So how does this happen? There are always the obvious
reasons—say, bad judgment, push-up bras, massive quantities
of Bud Light—but have you ever considered that you might
have multiple personalities? We've conducted a great deal of
research for this book, in places ranging from a carefully
selected cross-section of sleazy bars (Robin) to a variety of
AOL adult chat rooms (Jay), and we've come to the conclusion that every good Walk of Shame begins with something
we call Walk of Shame Personality Multiplication Syndrome
(WoS-PMS). This is a not-so-fancy way of saying that there
are two totally different versions of you. It just so happens
that one of them is really, really fond of Jell-O shots, has a
strange habit of dancing on tables, and once made out with a

guy with a fake German accent who said he was a professional skydiver. The other You: she's the one who occasionally pays the phone bill on time, and holy shit is she going to be pissed when some old guy in a bar recognizes her from a *Girls Gone Wild* video.

See, men understand this syndrome instinctively. That's why so many of them drink. For a lot of guys, drinking is the only way they can decisively bring out the one personality inside them that would willingly sleep with a woman dumb enough to have them. It's tricky, but they make it work.

But it's not just drinking that brings out the other You. Almost any stimulus can do the job: a meaningful glance, a too-tight dress, "The Thong Song," even a perfect back alley or a serious drug craving. As soon as the sun goes down, we are all of us in danger of transforming, going down on someone really unfortunate, and then having to take that long, long walk.

Here's the thing: we understand. Really, we do. So instead of curing cancer or mediating in the Middle East peace talks, we've put together this book—something to help you understand and cope with the shame. Just the shame, though: if you're experiencing any sort of rash, discharge, or painful urination, that's between you and the free clinic.

Another question we're often asked is this: "Who takes the Walk of Shame?" To which we respond, well: "Who *doesn't*?" We tried to make a list:

1. Judge Judy
2. Pope John Paul II (shame-free since 1967)
3. Robin's mom but not Jay's
4. Jessica Simpson
5. 72% of Amish people
6. Jared Fogle
7. Small children who don't live in West Virginia
8. Christopher Walken
9. Snoop Dogg is happily married
10. ???

The sick thing is that we blew almost a quarter of our beer budget just coming up with that. The point is this: the Walk of Shame doesn't discriminate, not based on age, class, race, creed, gender, or sexual orientation. Especially not on sexual orientation. Which is sort of reassuring, right? I mean, just imagine all the people who could be making that walk right along with you: Tara Reid! Kim Jong Il! Homeless guys! God bless America, and other countries, too.

Which means, yes, boys do take the Walk of Shame. I mean, you wouldn't know it from looking at them, but apparently it turns out that boys have feelings. Plus look at how poor their judgment is even *before* they start drinking. Do you think they have no shame in that? They are not animals. If you prick them, do they not bleed? If they do nine shots of Jägermeister and wake up in a room full of Hello Kitty products with a lazy-eyed girl they'll run into every Thursday morning in Econ, do they not sort of want to puke? If they have to stumble home to roommates who remember exactly which hatchet-faced but very large-breasted girl they offered to walk home the night before, do they not sort of want to just up and move instead? Jay says the answer to all of these rhetorical questions is a resounding "Yes," and that sometimes breasts at parties turn out to be smaller than they appear.

Besides, the level of teasing a girl's friends will give her over a good shameful hook-up is child's play compared to what boys will do. Boys have absolutely no sense of privacy, and not in the cute, gossipy "let's destroy her life" way, either. We've seen two guys wrestle one of their friends to the ground so they could *smell his fingers*, which turned out to smell more than a little like certain parts of an overly made-up Idaho girl named Ashley. Ashley would actually fall for that thing where you say, "Where are you *from*?" and she says "Idaho," and you say, "Yeah, I know, but where are you from?" You could do it to her over and over, but after the first ten times it stopped being funny and was really just sad.

Anyway, here's the most important part: the Walk of Shame isn't just for college kids. The bad news is that you could be taking the Walk of Shame well into your thirties. You may not in fact actually meet that dreamy boy who makes everything okay forever and ever, and you especially aren't going to meet him if you spend every weekend flashing people in a Kappa Sigma basement. Let's be honest: if you're doing the Walk now, chances are you'll be doing it for a while yet.

It won't get any easier, either. Sure, sure, maybe you'll get used to it. Maybe you'll get to the point where your Sunday-morning stumble-homes are so routine that your neighbors start thinking you go to some strange, slutty church. But all that means is that one day you'll be thirty-three and searching for your panties under some sleazy Eurotrash bartender's bed, and it'll all come crashing down on you: what the hell has gone wrong with your life that you don't even find this embarrassing anymore? Why in the world do you have fifteen years' worth of Walk of Shame experience and only five in direct-mail marketing, which has somehow become your career? And why are there eight different polka-dot thongs under here?

Of course, if you're a guy, we're going to have to accept that Jay is right: the Walk of Shame just gets better and better. Wait until you're half-bald and cruising home in your stupid little sports car with tell-tale stains all over the top half of your Dockers—you will totally feel like the man then. You'll be thumbs-upping truckers and whipping out your cell to call up all your skeezy friends and tell them how long it's been since you scored with a chick who's never given birth. Congratulations, asshole.

It's a daunting world out there. The good news—the really good news—is that we're here for you. And we're dedicating ourselves to one simple task: by the time you finish this book, you'll be the best little slut you can be.

Your Slutsign and You

Your first lesson is this: there are several different types of Walks of Shame. Some of them are very common, while others are less known and less appreciated. Your more typical Walks of Shame are a lot like the part of college where you go to classes and take exams: it's pretty much what you're *supposed* to do, now and then. But isn't college really more about the new people and things you experience *outside* the classroom? Isn't it really about broadening yourself? Some of the less common Walks of Shame can broaden you, too, in ways your gynecologist will notice but probably not say anything about.

What we've created here is a complete taxonomy of Walk of Shame types. You may find that you've experienced many of these Walk of Shame varieties—maybe even several at once, if you're into that. Think back far enough, though, and you'll likely realize that you always return to one key Walk of Shame type. This is what's known as your Slutsign. Knowing your Slutsign offers you the key to a much deeper understanding of yourself as a person, both emotionally and in terms of what kinds of bras you should wear.

To figure out the type of any given Walk of Shame, you need only answer the following two questions.

1. *How would you rate the hook-up itself?*

    a. Horrifying; you can't believe you spent the night with *that*.

    b. Average; another Saturday night, another awkward handjob.

    c. Hot Hot Hot; you're shopping for wedding dresses and/or bondage gear.

2. *How are you taking your Walk?*

    a. Covert; if anyone sees you, there's always the cyanide pill.

    b. Carefree; Walk of Shame? No, no, you've just been out all night clubbing.

    c. Shameless; if anyone happens to find your panties, could they let you know?

Now just plot your answers on this chart to find the matching Slutsign, or the associated male Slutsign subtype.

Your Slutsign and You				
YOUR HOOK-UP RATING				
		Horrifying	*Average*	*Hot Hot Hot*
Your Walking Style	*Covert*	**True Shame**	**The Priss** The Choir Boy	**The Secret Inferno** The Closet Case
	Carefree	**Party People**	**The Sophisticate** The Player	**The Lucky Bitch** The German
	Shameless	**The Ho** The Man-Ho	**The Harlot** The Braggart	**The Brazen Hussy** The Outright Liar

Let's examine each of these types in detail.

1. True Shame (Horrifying/Covert)

This, obviously, is the worst of all Walk of Shame types: you've just done something truly foul with someone really unfortunate, and trust us, everyone knows. No one believes you had an early-morning "meeting" with the girl who plays the tuba in marching band. It happens to everyone sooner or later, right? Well, sure—but if this is truly your Walk of Shame *type*, woe is you. It's one thing to get super-trashed and accidentally-on-purpose go down on that kid who always wears the fedora; it's a whole other thing to make a career out of it. If this is really your Slutsign—and deep down in your heart and/or genitals, you know whether it is or not—you've gone past simple bad judgment. This is who you *are* now.

Which leaves you with two options. If living True Shame is anything like alcoholism, then you need to take a look at yourself in the mirror, summon up all of your strength, and commit to changing your life. We don't recommend that, because fuck, who's got the time? Plus, truthfully, we kind of enjoy having people like you around when we're horny but don't smell so good. Our advice is to think of it more like being gay: you're here, you sleep with morons, we're all *more* than used to it. Accept yourself. Just ride it out until a really bad case of genital warts solves everything for you.

Famous individuals who share your Slutsign: Legend has it that Catherine the Great died when a horse she was having sex with fell on top of her. We figure this is the kind of

True Shame you'd really rather be dead for. **Patron school:** DeVry. **Look for:** The Man-Ho is good for providing absolute, never-ending shame; Party People will magically appear right when you're ready to do something stupid; and the Closet Case will convince you to try something particularly weird and regrettable. **Avoid:** The Braggart will tell everyone, and the Choirboy will call you every day for a week, "just to talk."

2. The Priss/The Choirboy (Average/Covert)

You went out and hooked up with a boy. He was cute, he was nice, he didn't try anything especially creepy, and you even harbor the delusion that he might call you back at some point. So why are you slinking home like nobody knows you even have a vagina?

Because you're a Priss, that's why. And you *do* have a vagina, even if you and your Choirboy counterparts would rather refer to it as a "coochie pop" or "kittycat" or "down *there*." It's not your fault: you were probably raised that way. Without drastic intervention, you'll stay that way, too. You'll wind up one of those middle-aged ladies who whisper to one another that Brad Pitt has "nice buns" and then giggle and go, "Oh, we're just *terrible*. Aren't we just so *terrible*?"

It's sort of our policy not to favor any one Slutsign over another, but really: if this is you, get a fucking grip. You know that knocking sound you keep hearing when you and your girlfriends are eating Häagen-Dazs and watching *Sex and the City* reruns and going on about how much you admire Samantha for being so liberated and spunky? That's the sound of your upstairs neighbor getting banged by her coked-up video-artist boyfriend. You're not "so terrible," you're an irritating little freak.

Famous individuals who share your Slutsign: George Orwell, Lacey Chabert, and Busta Rhymes. **Patron school:** Wheaton. **Look for:** Prisses should look for Party People and Players, both of whom will find their prissiness an amusing challenge for about four hours; Choirboys should look for Lucky Bitches, who will take great pleasure in mussing them up. **Avoid:** Nobody, you could use the experience.

3. The Secret Inferno/The Closet Case (Hot Hot Hot/Covert)

You really think you're a Secret Inferno? That's cool, that's nice. Have a seat, sweetie. My name's Jay. How you feeling, girl?

What you've got to realize is that I understand you, baby. I'm here for you. I know where you're coming from, you know? Let me guess: you were valedictorian of your high school, right? Or else one of those girls who rode horses. Your parents were all strict, right? Immigrants? I feel that, girl. It's like we've got this connection, you know?

Scoot in closer, I can't quite hear you. You never really had much experience with boys? That's cool. Let me guess—you went around rereading the smutty bondage parts from romance novels, right? Or else fantasizing about your Academic Decathlon coach? That's the one? Yeah, you see, Priya, it's like I really *get* you, you know?

Hold up girl, you got something on your shirt. What is this, cashmere? Feels nice.

See, I know what's happening to you these days. Tell me if I'm wrong. Every time you get your hands on an actual man, right, you turn into someone else. Someone filthy. I feel that. He makes some kind of offhand joke, right, about how you deserve a spanking, and then suddenly you look all uncomfortable and you're like, well, I *guess* we could try that, if you really want to. And after that, it's all over. No, that's cool, sweetie, I understand: you're just a sexual person, right? Check it out: I even understand your shame. It's got nothing to do with the Walk itself, you know what I'm saying? You're just ashamed by all the ridiculous shit that you—a high school valedictorian, right—found yourself doing last night. I know, I know, that's deep, right? I swear, it's like we've got this unspoken connection. You feeling that, girl?

Let me get you another drink, princess.

See, I can help you, baby. I can help you break the cycle. I know how it goes: you get wrapped up in something all kinky, then you swear up and down that you'll never touch a boy again, and then, three weeks later, all of that repressed skank comes exploding out. Repressed sexuality, I mean. Am I right? So here's what you've got to do: when you've got that fourth shot in your hand, and you feel those urges bubbling up, you've got to call me. Any time, day or night. Put this number in your cell, girl. It's Jay, J-A-Y. After all we've been through, girl, you've got to trust me. I can help you through, you know?

Now, for the rest of the ladies, I usually give this advice about the Closet Cases: you've got to watch out for these guys. It's not a gay thing. These are just guys who've spent every waking minute since they were fourteen fantasizing about doing something really weird, like getting put in diapers or spanked with a dildo or something. But see, they're all tormented and ashamed about it. They're going to put all this charm into getting you to do it, right, and then they're never going to be able to look you in the eye again. Like, even if you were totally into it. Plus he's going to spend the rest of his life worrying that you told everyone about his Smurfs fantasy.

Don't go there.

Famous individuals who share your Slutsign: Mandy Moore and one of the Gore sisters, according to my brother's old roommate's cousin's sponsor's best friend. Also Henry James. **Patron school:** Sarah Lawrence. **Look for:** Lucky Bitches and Germans can help guide you into a healthy world of accepting your filthiness; other Secret Infernos and Closet Cases, on the other hand, can help create dramatic cycles of double-kinkiness, which you should also come to me for help with. **Avoid:** Sophisticates and Players are some of the most boring, unimaginative people you could ever sleep with.

4. Party People (Horrifying/Carefree)

Party People in the house! You guys: you're the vast unappreciated working class of the Walk of Shame. So what if you don't get all flashy, picking up hip, attractive people and having marginally satisfying sex with them? So what if your hook-ups usually start with clumsy, idiotic groping and usually end with someone throwing up? You're the ones down there in the trenches, every weekend, finishing off the cheaper beer and offering to walk drunk girls home. You're the grunts, the patriots, the people who make it all happen—and for that, we salute you.

Unfortunately, we're also obliged to inform you that you're totally bottom of the barrel, hotness-wise. If you look at the middle row of the Slutsign chart, you'll notice a pretty clear pecking order—and you guys, sad to say, are on the business end of it. This leaves you with two options. The first is to embrace the pecking order, and do everything in your power to move upward. Buy some better clothes, get to know the right people, and you might be able to bluff your way into becoming a player, playa. Spread a vague rumor about how you can deep-throat a can of Sprite, and you might develop enough intrigue to say you're a Sophisticate. You will never, ever be a Lucky Bitch or a German, but hey, during those first few weeks of school, the freshmen are still too dumb to know the difference.

Or you can go with the second option: revolution. After all, who are these Players and Lucky Bitches to look down on *you*? Majoring in communications, wearing sweatshirts all the time, liking the Dave Matthews Band—it doesn't make you a bad *person*, does it? Having played high school volleyball, being your dorm's student government representative for three years running, having that same stupid Manet print as every other girl in the hall—it doesn't make you any worse in bed, does it? Remember: you're the one who's *there*, every weekend, flirting with computer science boys and explaining to people how you've been "thinking about" smoking weed for the first time. You're the front line. You're the real America, Party People, and we wish you the best.

Famous individuals who share your Slutsign: Britney Spears, Britney Spears, and Britney Spears. **Patron school:** Ohio State. **Look for/Avoid:** Like it matters to you?

5. The Sophisticate/The Player (Average/Carefree)

You think you're pretty cool, right? I mean, there you are, right smack in the middle of the pecking order: maybe you're not as supernaturally cool as those weirdo Lucky Bitches and Germans, but you're certainly not some kind of pleb Party Person, either. You know your way around; you know what you're up to. You can pick over a crowd and get your hands on someone good, someone desirable. Because *you're* desirable. You've got your friends at your side, and the world is mostly your oyster.

Here's the bad news: nobody likes you. Which is fine—you'll get laid either way. We just thought you should know:

nobody likes you. Even all those people who are willing to hook up with you—they don't really like you, either. They *know* how corny and arrogant you are, because you're totally transparent, but all they really care about is that you're cute and you seem to have done this before. It's win-win. It's like, Sophisticates: most of the guys who get with you find you shallow and irritating. It's just that they have ulterior motives. Half the time they figure you're used to getting with guys who won't return your phone calls, which saves them a lot of energy. The rest of the time, they were sitting around with their friends talking about how you're *so* lame but have a super-nice ass, and now they want to impress everyone by talking about how they got on you. And then, in the rare cases that you get with a super-fine, in-demand player, well, you might want to sit down: it turns out he's only making out with you as a "favor" to your pledge mother.

No offense.

Famous individuals who share your Slutsign: Nelly, Arnold Schwarzenegger, Nietzsche. **Patron schools:** Columbia, boys at Vassar. **Look for:** Other Sophisticates and Players are obvious, since you've all been gaming one another since day one; Prisses are a fun pseudo-challenge for Players; and in a pinch, Harlots, Braggarts, and Hos are always easy pickings.

Avoid: Lucky Bitches and Germans will have absolutely nothing to do with you, and may even go out of their way to make you feel insipid. And if you're backsliding into getting with Party People, you may need to face the fact that you're probably becoming one of them.

6. The Lucky Bitch / The German (Hot Hot Hot / Carefree)

There's only one kind of woman who can go out for drinks, pick up a guy who's male-modeling his way through med school, have the most torrid encounter since Reconstruction, and then stroll absentmindedly home like she's just been out buying dishwashing liquid. This kind of woman is known as the Lucky Bitch.

Most women aren't very fond of the Lucky Bitch. This is perfectly fine with the Lucky Bitch, because she has an endless supply of hot male friends—you wouldn't know them—who think she's the greatest person on Earth. Which, frankly, she is. She gets along with everyone, and you always see her having lunch with the cuter professors. She knows more about music and film than you do. Most of those hot-guy friends are in bands, and only show up when they're playing in town. Don't worry—she'll e-mail you about their show.

That's the problem. Everything would be fine if she just had the decency to be a stuck-up cunt about it. But she's always so pleasant and charming, and thinks you should do your hair like *this*, because you're so *beautiful*. In conclusion: she is a stupid wench.

The male equivalent of the Lucky Bitch is known as the German, because in seventy percent of cases he is, indeed, German. In the remaining thirty percent of cases he is either Austrian, Dutch, half-Parsee, or the son of an American diplomat. The German can be recognized by his incredible height, his designer shoes, and the fact that he is perpetually running late for a drug-filled hipster house party being thrown by some Bulgarians he went to prep school with. This fact will make him seem all the more intriguing and starlike when he shows up to a kegger in a fraternity basement. He'll lean casually against a wall, looking all hot and serene, and then, if you're lucky, he'll step outside with you for a smoke and tell you fascinating stories about how much cooler Prague was when he was fourteen.

Think this may be your Slutsign? It's not. A true Lucky Bitch or German would have put this book down after reading like three sentences, because some hot Japanese people called about this great warehouse party.

Famous individuals who share your Slutsign: This is a trick question, because the whole point of being a famous person is to seem like a Lucky Bitch/German. **Patron schools:** NYU (film and theater departments); New School; UCSD. **Look for:** Other Lucky Bitches and Germans, almost exclusively—along with the occasional Secret Inferno or Closet Case, who may, with some counseling, become Lucky Bitches or Germans themselves. Lucky Bitches may also fall in love with and marry Choirboys, because they're cute when they're so uptight. **Avoid:** Party People are to you as Keystone Light is to champagne. And don't even talk to Sophisticates or Players: they'll start thinking they're one of you, and onlookers might assume you're becoming one of them. Spend lots of time consoling True Shamers, sort of in the same way middle-class people worry about the homeless but wouldn't dream of sleeping with them.

---

7. The Ho/The Man-Ho (Horrifying/Shameless)

Damn, girl, you nasty. Everyone already knows what being a ho is all about, so we won't embarrass you by going into it. We hope you'll enjoy the following anecdote, which we're including instead.

See, back when Jay and I were just little bitty students at

a major midwestern college, we knew this homeless guy named Alonzo. Alonzo was a real nice guy, but you could see why he was homeless: this guy spent three years trying to get into the business of selling shitty weed to college students, and he couldn't even get that off of the ground. So one day, at this one Burger King, Alonzo comes up to Jay and just asks, flat-out, "You ever get a blowjob from a woman with no teeth?" And we were all a little creeped-out by the fact that Jay *thought* about it before he said no.

Anyway, for the record: this is an experience Alonzo particularly recommends. So like a few days later, Jay's getting off of a train right around where Alonzo hangs out, and there's this really old woman sitting there with a cup. So Jay walks over and tosses a quarter in, and the old woman smiles at him, AND SHE HAS NO TEETH! AND THERE WAS A HOOK ON THE DOOR HANDLE! That's how Jay tells stories, it's really irritating.

The point is that you, Ho, have got nothing on that woman.

Famous individuals who share your Slutsign: Tara Reid, Bruce Willis, Lenin, Jenna Bush, Ann Coulter, David Guest, Pamela Anderson, Milan Kundera, Pocahontas, and Fran Drescher. **Patron schools:** Florida, Florida State, Miami,

UNLV, Ohio Athens, Texas A&M, Nebraska, and UCLA.
Look for/Avoid: Surely the whole point here is that you'll
sleep with pretty much anyone.

8. The Harlot/The Braggart (Average/Shameless)

The weird thing about Harlots and Braggarts is that they
come in two very different varieties—one that's great and one
that sucks. The only thing the two types have in common is
that they're both totally happy to tell you all about every
single person they've ever humped. After that, though, they
start heading in opposite directions.

For instance, the good kind of Harlot is the girl who'll
take you to a party, introduce you around the room, and then
tell you really great details about all the guys you just passed:
that one's uncircumcised, that one's got a third nipple, that
one makes really goofy noises if you lick him in the right
place. The bad kind of Harlot is the girl who calls you up,
invites you out for coffee, and then goes on and on about how
she's dating this cute new guy, he's a law student, and the sex
is totally great, only she worries that he's less experienced than
her, plus the other night she wound up sleeping with Brad
again, and Brad's really blah blah blah. Seriously, if this bitch
is you, then you need to either (a) fuck off and die already, or

at least (b) stop sitting right next to me at the coffee shop and yakking into your cell phone about how, well, you probably had *more* orgasms with Dean, but the orgasms you have with Andrew are probably *better*.

When it comes to Braggarts, the key is self-awareness. I mean, some guys can tell you loads of stories about chicks they've gotten on, and yet somehow keep the whole thing from being a total cliché. It takes modesty, insight, and good comic timing, but it's possible. Unfortunately, most Braggarts aren't even close to pulling that off. Most Braggarts just single out really incredibly average or even somewhat plain girls, and then jab you in the ribs and start winking and making implications. A lot of the time they use terms like "johnson" or "bumping uglies," though most of the time they just fall back on "if you know what I mean." And we do know what they mean. That's why we're huddled up in corners trying to gouge our own brains out just to keep from picturing it.

Famous people who share your Slutsign: Cher, Madonna, Katha Pollitt, and Charles Dickens. **Patron schools:** Wesleyan for the good kind; Evergreen, Notre Dame, and Northwestern's theater department for the bad. **Look for:** This gets complicated. The role of a good Harlot is to work through every Player around, collecting dirt. The role of the bad Harlot is to try and interest you in their boring relationships with Party People and Choirboys. The role of a good Braggart is to expose people to True Shame and then tell comical stories about it. The role of a bad Braggart is to think he's scoring with Sophisticates when he's really scraping the bottom of the Party People barrel. **Avoid:** Anyone who still believes there's anything remotely special about sex?

9. The Brazen Hussy/The Outright Liar (Hot Hot Hot/Shameless)

Cheers to you, bitch: Brazen Hussies kick serious ass. What's great about you guys is that—unlike, say, a lot of Harlots—you don't think there's anything cool or liberated or lifestylish about getting laid all the time and then telling everyone about it. It's just what you do. Which is exactly how you manage to score such hot guys. You don't even have to be cute: they just talk to you for a half hour and they can *tell* you've got special skills. You can even get away with being mean, or boring, since having intellectual conversations with you is *so* not the point.

Your male counterparts, on the other hand, suck ass. Wait, we got that backwards—*you* suck ass, if asked politely. Your male counterparts just suck, more generally. Because look: any guy who goes around telling everyone how he just had a threesome with some cheerleaders is clearly not a guy cheerleaders would ever have a threesome with. Same goes for that guy who keeps a blog about all of the TAs he's dated.

In conclusion: Brazen Hussies rule, Outright Liars drool.

Famous individuals who share your Slutsign: Lindsay Lohan, Henry Miller, Steve Harvey, Donald Rumsfeld, and Connie Chung. **Patron Schools:** Drake, Oberlin. **Look for:** Brazen Hussies fare well with Germans and, especially, Man-Hos; any women who would actually get on an Outright Liar are immediately remanded to the True Shame category. **Avoid:** Prisses make good friends and admirers for Brazen Hussies, but Choirboys are a poor romantic choice. Outright Liars should avoid Secret Infernos, because the one time their outrageous stories turn out to be true, no one will believe them—a sure path toward misery, psychosis, and possibly suicide. Sorry to end on a downer like that.

Your Horoscope

Now that you know and understand the Slutsigns that control your destiny—and really, seriously, they do—the next step is to look to the stars, the slutty ones, and learn important, sexy things about the future. (The slutty stars, in our experience, are Sirius, Alpha Centauri, the sticky bit of the Little Dipper, and at least four of the Seven Sisters.)

Now let's get one thing straight: we've put a whole lot of time and energy into creating and double-checking every one of these horoscopes. We had to go to the planetarium and everything, and not even on one of those laser light show nights. So don't even dream of doing *anything* without consulting these pages first. It will turn out badly and we will laugh.

January

True Shame: Beware of a small black man with a limp. He is not really a professional basketball player, and you should totally know that.

The Priss/The Choirboy: Start the year with a bang! The stars really want to watch.

The Secret Inferno/The Closet Case: January will be an excellent month for your finances. Unfortunately, March will be a terrible month for learning that all those videos you sold violated several Alabama state decency laws.

Party People: Don't worry—that hangover won't really last all month. Vigorous masturbation on the 23rd will leave you feeling fit as a fiddle once again.

The Sophisticate/The Player: Romance will enter your life in the form of an older man or woman. Remember: the nursing home has an eleven o'clock curfew.

The Lucky Bitch/The German: Keep your thoughts positive. On or around the 15th you will have a spectacularly good hair day.

The Ho/The Man-Ho: You will get crabs.

The Harlot/The Braggart: Just as you are sitting down to finish an important project, both of your grandmothers will die in unrelated boating accidents. And no, no one will believe you.

The Brazen Hussy/The Outright Liar: The stars say you should avoid a man with a strange birthmark on his scrotum. Only they're not sure how you can avoid him once you've already seen the birthmark. Just don't lick it, whatever you do.

February

True Shame: You will spend Valentine's Day curled up in a corner vomiting yourself to sleep, having learned three separate lessons about the advisability of drinking Mexican champagne.

The Priss/The Choirboy: You will spend Valentine's Day on a date with someone your parents introduced you to. The stars don't need to tell you how lame that is.

The Secret Inferno/The Closet Case: Your Valentine's Day will be ruined by a malfunctioning ball gag.

Party People: You will spend Valentine's Day pretending that chubby girl from your dorm is actually interesting. The stars say she's not.

The Sophisticate/The Player: If in doubt about whom

to ask out for Valentine's Day, here's a handy rule of thumb: breast/penis size.

The Lucky Bitch/The German: You will spend Valentine's Day listening to Kimiko go on and on and on about Travis's weird clown fetish. If you don't know anyone named Kimiko or Travis, don't worry: you will.

The Ho/The Man-Ho: You will spend Valentine's Day with crabs.

The Harlot/The Braggart: You will spend Valentine's Day under the mistaken impression that lederhosen are the cool new thing.

The Brazen Hussy/The Outright Liar: You will spend Valentine's Day in the hospital. Other people may believe that it was appendicitis, but remember: the stars know all, and they really hope you don't plan on ever using that spatula again.

March

True Shame: March is the perfect month for trying something new. The stars suggest self-respect.

The Priss/The Choirboy: Your inability to speak Urdu may prove to be a problem. Learn Urdu. Specifically, learn the words for "monkey," "stapler," "emergency," and "please."

The Secret Inferno/The Closet Case: Kids today are so strange, aren't they? Try not to get too excited about that.

Party People: This month you will learn a new sexual position, one you never previously imagined could exist. You won't enjoy it, and it may even hurt a little. Sorry.

The Sophisticate/The Player: The stars refer you to the immortal wisdom of Bel Biv Devoe: never trust a big butt and a smile. Unless you can afford long-term hospitalization following an exhilarating buttcrack-suffocation accident on the 8th.

The Lucky Bitch/The German: Be mean to people this month. The stars don't indicate that there's any advantage to that, but it'll totally be fun.

The Ho/The Man-Ho: Expect a financial loss around the 12th, when you finally buy the new sheets and prescription shampoos necessary to get rid of those crabs.

The Harlot/The Braggart: The plight of the homeless is a truly tragic thing. By the end of the month you will have learned that marrying them doesn't help.

The Brazen Hussy/The Outright Liar: You will meet a former cast member from *Degrassi Junior High*. Use a condom.

April

True Shame: Due to a lapse in your birth-control prescription, you will develop a revolutionary new multiple-partner rhythm method.

The Priss/The Choirboy: Consider getting a pet. You're totally boring on your own.

The Secret Inferno/The Closet Case: April is the month to follow your dreams. Unfortunately you can't just *go* to jail without having committed a crime. Also, unlike what you see on Cinemax, they don't actually hose down the female prisoners.

Party People: You will waste three hundred dollars on a last-minute flight to Houston for the sole purpose of joining the Mile High Club. Shortly afterward, you will learn that Delta really *does* hire transsexual flight attendants.

The Sophisticate/The Player: This month's sperm donation will allow your grandchildren to unknowingly enjoy some mega-hot incest action.

The Lucky Bitch/The German: You will join a touring company of *Naked Cats*.

The Ho/The Man-Ho: The best month of your year: no crabs!

The Harlot/The Braggart: Before your Model UN panel on the 18th, try to learn the actual meaning of the word "concubine."

The Brazen Hussy/The Outright Liar: If you're having trouble telling whether dinner on the 28th is a meeting or a date, try grabbing the woman's crotch. If bail is set at under $3000, it was probably a date.

May

True Shame: You will wake up naked and wet in the backseat of a limousine, but that guy from the *Police Academy* movies will never give you the $200 he promised.

The Priss/The Choirboy: You will menstruate this month. Psych!

The Secret Inferno/The Closet Case: You will meet a tall, handsome Bulgarian girl.

Party People: Look, the stars have really enjoyed getting to know you, but don't you think you'd both be happier if you took a little break from each other?

The Sophisticate/The Player: You will accidentally sleep with one of those guys who compares everything that happens to a *Seinfeld* plot.

The Lucky Bitch/The German: You will accidentally sleep with one of those girls who compares everything that happens to an episode of *Friends*. Try and convince her that there was one where Ross and Rachel tied each other up and had anal sex.

The Ho/The Man-Ho: You will get crabs again.

The Harlot/The Braggart: Big breasts aren't everything. The ass is important, too. A bizarre surgical accident on the 9th will ensure that you have way more than enough of both.

The Brazen Hussy/The Outright Liar: May is the perfect month to try Internet dating. Psych yourself up by imagining all the hot dirty things you'll be able to say in bed, stuff like "Oh, yeah, cyberindigo, give it to me, k thanx bye."

June

True Shame: No, it's not you: it really is hot in here. Get over yourself.

The Priss/The Choirboy: Watch your weight toward the middle of the month. Now do you understand the difference between an exponential increase and a geometric one?

The Secret Inferno/The Closet Case: Your friends and family will finally make you realize that no, your mail-order bride doesn't look anything like Heather Locklear. Not even around the eyes. Heather Locklear is not Laotian.

Party People: Your training for next year's naked 5K run will hit an unexpected snag. Actually it's less of a "snag" and more of a "rusty protruding nail."

The Sophisticate/The Player: Doctors will use your case to confirm that there really is such a thing as "tanorexia."

The Lucky Bitch/The German: Forewarned is forearmed! On the 12th, duck.

The Ho/The Man-Ho: You will suffer heartbreak at the end of the month. Take some small comfort in the fact that you gave the dude crabs.

The Harlot/The Braggart: On or around the 10th, you will marry Jennifer Lopez.

The Brazen Hussy/The Outright Liar: On or around the 28th, you will marry Jennifer Lopez.

July

True Shame: Your parents will reunite, brought together again by their shared disappointment in you.

The Priss/The Choirboy: You may or may not be torn limb from limb by a sex-mad *Oprah* audience. It all depends on which pair of shorts you wear.

The Secret Inferno/The Closet Case: Look forward to a hot mid-month romance with a redhead. Like an Irish Terrier, maybe.

Party People: Your lucky number this month is pi. Not "pie," lardass, "pi."

The Sophisticate/The Player: Your fraternity-hazing wounds will finally heal, leaving you fresh and ready for a whole new round of homoerotic spankings.

The Lucky Bitch/The German: Dude, *nobody* likes dreadlocks.

The Ho/The Man-Ho: July is the month for soul-searching. Start here: what the hell has gone wrong with your life, and why do you still have crabs?

The Harlot/The Braggart: A friend will come to you for advice. Soon afterward, she will casually mention that sleeping with you seems to be your solution for everything.

The Brazen Hussy/The Outright Liar: Help the stars help you: stop killing hobos. It's fun now, but it'll surely end in tragedy.

August

True Shame: You know how in that one commercial they can superglue the furniture to the ceiling? It turns out to really work, but you'll learn soon enough why that doesn't really save space.

The Priss/The Choirboy: Man cannot live on bread alone. This month you will learn that man cannot live on bread and pickles alone, either.

The Secret Inferno/The Closet Case: You will become paranoid that Steve Harvey is lurking in your closet. Stop listening to the smooth jazz station, and you'll feel much better.

Party People: You will have sex with the woman of your dreams. Incidentally, this month you will have a terrible recurring dream about Lynne Cheney.

The Sophisticate/The Player: Try to stay positive this month. When you're ugly and smell horrible, it takes a very upbeat attitude to make friends.

The Lucky Bitch/The German: The best way to keep your roommate from spying on you in the bathroom is to go on that all-asparagus diet you've been hearing about.

The Ho/The Man-Ho: You will find true love! Just kidding.

The Harlot/The Braggart: How many roads must a man walk down, before they call him a man? In your case, just one more: the headline will read "Area Man Killed by Bus."

The Brazen Hussy/The Outright Liar: Actually, you're not crazy. Paris Hilton really *does* want to have sex with you. You should be flattered, there's only like a one in a hundred chance of that happening.

September

True Shame: If you happen to find an eight-ball of coke in your apartment, could you call the stars' friend Eddie? He's pretty sure he had sex with you at some point.

The Priss/The Choirboy: September is totally too late to jump on the whole trucker-hat trend. Unless you're somehow reading this in September of 1999.

The Secret Inferno/The Closet Case: You will meet an incredible man who loves your personality. Don't you wish you were gay?

Party People: You know how Vincent van Gogh cut off his ear and gave it to a chick? Around the 17th you should try to remember it didn't actually get him any.

The Sophisticate/The Player: You will go on eight dates with a kinky food critic before finally standing up for yourself and refusing to let him eat Salisbury steak off of your ass.

The Lucky Bitch/The German: Trust your instincts. They're absolutely right: a mammogram isn't supposed to involve cocoa butter.

The Ho/The Man-Ho: You will find true love! For real this time. Then this person will discover you have crabs.

The Harlot/The Braggart: If you're really thinking of being a sexy nurse for Halloween, you should probably stop eating entirely by the 2nd.

The Brazen Hussy/The Outright Liar: Your mother loves you very much. A little *too* much, actually. Let her down gently.

October

True Shame: No matter what they tell you in Tijuana, that's not what "chimichanga" means.

The Priss/The Choirboy: Jenna Elfman is really irritating, but the stars just want to mention that she has kind of a killer body.

The Secret Inferno/The Closet Case: How many times do the stars have to tell you? Stop having sex with your cousin already.

Party People: Everyone at the gala will love your elegant reinterpretation of the Cabbage Patch.

The Sophisticate/The Player: You will be selected as a contestant in a new reality-show competition called *Who Wants to Suck Off a Hundredaire?* Seriously, that's what the camera is for.

The Lucky Bitch/The German: The stars can think of eight good reasons why you shouldn't get breast implants. Reason number five: you're a *guy*.

The Ho/The Man-Ho: See March.

The Harlot/The Braggart: Remember: diamonds are a girl's best friend. Second best? The morning-after pill.

The Brazen Hussy/The Outright Liar: The stars aren't sure why those men have suddenly stopped picking up your trash. Maybe if you fixed yourself up a little?

November

True Shame: If you want to let everyone know you're gay, there are better ways than buying a tiger.

The Priss/The Choirboy: Two words: anal beads. You'll know what the stars mean when the time comes.

The Secret Inferno/The Closet Case: A job interview will go horribly wrong due to a bra malfunction. You'll get the job, though.

Party People: Plastic surgery will leave your nose looking disturbingly like a penis. But don't worry, that's not why everyone calls you "dickface."

The Sophisticate/The Player: Your boyfriend's not cheating on you. It's just that a snake bit his penis, and the first twelve girls couldn't manage to suck out the venom.

The Lucky Bitch/The German: Midway through the trial you will break down crying and reveal your incestuous relationship with your great-uncle Skip. Nevertheless, you will still be held responsible for that speeding ticket.

The Ho/The Man-Ho: A tall, charismatic man will try to lure you into an insane evangelical cult. We say go for it.

The Harlot/The Braggart: Your eighth and final viewing

of *The Care Bears Movie* will finally reveal its blatant homoerotic subtext.

The Brazen Hussy/The Outright Liar: You know what's a really good baby name? D'Jesus. It works for boys *or* girls.

December

True Shame: Everyone farts. Not necessarily as much as you're going to this month, and not during sex, but still.

The Priss/The Choirboy: On the off chance that you spend December marooned on a desert island with Colin Farrell, could you let him know that the lab called, and yes, it turns out those really are genital warts?

The Secret Inferno/The Closet Case: Don't worry about the underwear you lost last night: Hanukkah is coming!

Party People: Your new retro seventies look will have you picking chest hair out of your teeth in no time flat.

The Sophisticate/The Player: Don't lie on your résumé: there was nothing therapeutic about those massages.

The Lucky Bitch/The German: Try to get through the month without having sex. Learn to play the piano, or something. The stars are getting sick of all your canoodling.

The Ho/The Man-Ho: This month you probably just want to know if you're pregnant. The answer is no: guys can't get pregnant.

The Harlot/The Braggart: Your teenage fantasies of a department-store Santa gangbang will go unfulfilled. But the elves, the elves will be almost as good.

The Brazen Hussy/The Outright Liar: Congratulations on your pregnancy. This means seven generations have passed since the gypsy set that curse: all clear!

Other Voices

A Word for College Students
by Art Schnabel
Regional Sales Director, CosmoLube, Incorporated

Hi. I'm Art Schnabel, regional sales director for CosmoLube, Incorporated—here with a brief message for all of you out there in our nation's fine institutions of higher learning. Here at CosmoLube, we believe there's nothing more important than a first-class education. That's why we've contributed over six million dollars to the CosmoLube Inner City Scholarship Fund—to help make sure *every* student has the opportunity and the tools to seize his or her dreams. We're proud of every single one of our scholarship recipients, and we're proud of you, too. You, my friends, are the leaders of the future, and the things you're learning now will help create a better, happier future for you, your family, and our wonderful country.

But I'm here to let you in on a little secret: the things you learn in college aren't just limited to the lectures and the textbooks. This is your chance to grow as a human being—to stand up on your own two feet and figure out what sort of person you are and want to be. You'll experience a lot of important things in your time outside the classroom—and it's our sincere hope that as you experience these things, expanding your mind and developing as a mature, independent person, you'll be doing it all with the help of one of our fine CosmoLube products.

For instance, college-aged women may experience both physical urges and social pressure to engage in sexual activity. Remember: you're an adult now, and how you choose to respond to those urgings is entirely up to you. Our advice is to go with your heart and your gut; your body will always tell you what you are and aren't ready for. "But Art," you ask, "what if I'm pretty sure my body is wrong? What if it's not responding in quite the way I want it to?" Never fear: that's why we've developed CosmoLube's original "Glide-Wet" formula—so you'll always be ready to express your love in comfort and style. The more you use, the better you'll feel.

Those of you already in adult sexual relationships may find yourselves tempted to experiment with new forms of intimacy. Here at CosmoLube, we encourage this form of sexual expression. That's why we offer a wide variety of flavored and scented lubricants, from "Raspberry Cherry" to "Pina Colada Slicker" to "Hot Black Liquorice BootyLube." Try all of our exciting products—they're sure to add spice to your love life. And for an even richer, more intimate experience, there's nothing quite like a round of well-lubricated anal sex. Just remember to take it slow, and use at least one full bottle of CosmoLube's dependable "Loose Caboose" formula.

But exploring your sexuality isn't just for women, now, is it? All the men out there should look forward to an equally exciting four years of personal growth—with CosmoLube's fine products helping you all along the way. Just imagine all the possibilities, all of the wonderful things that could happen in your life during your time as a student. We encourage you to explore every aspect of your sexuality. For instance, have you ever been with another man? There's no better time to try it—with a nice thick coating of CosmoLube's new "Manhole Cover" formula, you just might like what you find. Be prepared for anything. And if you find yourself temporarily without an intimate partner, don't worry too much:

there are many different forms of sexual expression you can engage in on your own. Pick up a bottle of CosmoLube's patented "Solo Flyer," and you'll be happy for weeks to come.

We here at CosmoLube wish you the best during your time in college. You'll remember these years forever as the time that made you who you are—and you just might remember them as the best years of your life. Here's hoping they're educational, motivating, life-changing, and very well lubricated.

Art Schnabel

Regional Sales Director
CosmoLube, Incorporated

The Walk of Shame Calendar

*A*hh, the passing of the seasons. The rich pageant of nature. And oh, the festivals and holidays with which we mere mortals mark the days, the days ticking endlessly away toward our own deaths! Yep, the calendar year is a pretty special thing.

The progress of the year will also mark significant changes in the style and method of your Walk of Shame. That's why we've assembled the following calendar, so you'll always know how to take your Walk in a fashion that's sane, sensible, and appropriate.

January 1

The year sure starts with a bang: this is the second-best Walk of Shame day in the entire year. What with all the staying up late, getting drunk, and ritualized midnight kissing, we estimate that a full forty-eight percent of the American population kicks the year off with a serious—and seriously hungover—Walk of Shame. Why not embrace that fact? This is the one morning all year when it's perfectly normal to walk around looking like total shit, puking in nearby greenery, and scratching lubricant out of your crotch.

Winter

This season, depending on where you live, can be either the best or the worst possible time to take a Walk of Shame. If you live somewhere cold, you're in luck: chances are you won't be leaving the house without a thick, long jacket—and in the morning, the only serious indicator of your condition will be the smeared makeup and blotchy skin visible above your neck. If you live somewhere slightly warmer, look out. You will almost certainly cave to the pressure of going out at night without a coat, based on the irrefutable logic that if you wear a coat, other pedestrians will not be able to see your tits. You may, however, regret this choice in the morning. As you shiver your way home in a halter top and fishnet stockings, you won't just look like a workaday slut—you'll look like a refugee from the civil war in Skankistan.

February 15

Another important day in the yearly Walk of Shame cycle. If you're lucky, you'll wake up happily in the arms of someone who loves you, or at least doesn't plan on kicking you out of the apartment. But if you're anything like most people, you will spend at least two of the ten day-after-Valentine's-Days of your twenties waking up and realizing that you have been driven by loneliness and despair to do something really, really stupid. If you're feeling terrible about your life on the fourteenth, trust us: stay out of the bars. You will get drunk and maudlin and wind up crying yourself to sleep in the arms of a guy who you won't see again for three years, when you'll flick on the television and learn that all those missing hikers turned up in his basement.

Spring

Spring is an excellent season for the Walk of Shame. First of all, better weather means more parties—and now, barring rain, you'll be free to wander from one to another, looking for someone who's actually *worth* getting with. Second of all, if you're a college student, the year is winding down. Everyone's had a good seven or eight months to figure out what everyone else is up to. Everyone already knows who you have and haven't managed to hook up with, and what you did with them, and where you did it. The time for first impressions is long gone: you can just be yourself now. As you make your way home from that dorm where all the band geeks live, why not stop and smell the flowers? And so long as you're stopping, there appears to be some kind of clarinet reed stuck to your ass.

Easter

Nothing warms our hearts quite like the sight of children in their adorable Easter outfits, searching high and low for eggs and other hidden treats. Listen: on the off chance that you go out Saturday night and drink way too much, try not to pass out behind a bush, okay? And if you absolutely *have* to wind up back there, don't leave any condoms lying around. Do it for the kids, you know?

Mother's Day

Another fine Sunday holiday—and another Saturday on which to exercise some judgment. Do you really want to rush home all knock-kneed and get there just in time to give a holiday call to your *mother*? Set a drink minimum for the night before: two beers and out.

Summer

The whole trick to the summer Walk of Shame is wardrobe, wardrobe, wardrobe. The weather will be fine and balmy, and so you'll be tempted to break out your most extravagant, revealing outfits—to step out in style and turn heads. Resist this temptation. After all, it's summer, and everyone's feeling laid back. Unless you're totally ugly, you'll be able to flirt just as effectively in something casual, like a tiny pair of shorts and an overtight T-shirt. The advantage of the summer casuals? Wake up in the morning, wash off all your makeup, and trot casually back home: everyone will think you've just been out on a morning jog.

July 4

The birth of our nation gives us the opportunity to discuss something that definitely needs discussing: barbecue sex. Barbecues, as you may have noticed, tend to take place in yards and on decks. And with everyone drunk and outside—retreating only occasionally to the empty house to use the facilities—it often happens that two people disappear briefly inside and wind up sharing a drunken make-out moment in a silent, empty bedroom. All of which leads, inevitably, to what we'll call Barbecue Shame—the point where you both emerge, lips puffy and clothes misbuttoned, onto the active, happy deck. As a phenomenon it's certainly not restricted to barbecues: how often, at house parties, have you noticed two people slipping bashfully out of a back bedroom, and then coincidentally both deciding that they should really get home and go to bed early? Always, always watch yourself.

August

This, friends, is a dull month. If you live anyplace where it snows a lot, you'll probably end up going to a whole lot of birthday parties—winter sex, and all—but other than that, not much is happening. If you're a college student, it's quite likely that everyone you know is gone; if you're gainfully employed, it's quite likely that everyone you know is away on vacation. Every exciting thing you had planned for the summer has either already been accomplished or proved itself impossible. This is why you must remain ever-vigilant about August Shame. There's a lowering of standards that goes on. You're bored, right? And nobody you *actually* like seems to be in town. Soon enough you find yourself sitting out drinking beer with people you wouldn't even nod hello to during the academic year, and sooner or later you start to imagine that these people might actually be really great in bed. Just remember: August Shame isn't limited to the morning after. Come September, when things are getting back into their swing, a whole lot of conversations will revolve around what—and who—you did over the summer. Everyone else had exciting vacations in eastern Europe. Do you really want it to sound like you spent the whole time humping rejects?

Autumn

With the coming of autumn comes the return of the hustle and bustle of our nation's college campuses, ground zero for True Shame mornings. With the coming of autumn also comes a fresh batch of clueless college freshman, ready by their first parentless weekend to get really drunk and do horrible, horrible things they will still be regretting when they get their doctorates. Just remember: pace yourself. Back in spring, we said your time for first impressions was over. Toward the end of September, well, it's just begun.

November 1

And here we come to our absolute favorite Walk of Shame moment of the entire year: the day after Halloween! I don't know if you've noticed, but Halloween costumes in America seem to have taken a blasphemous turn for the whorish. After all, this holiday is supposed to be about the spirit world, the world of the dead, so why the *hell* does every girl between the ages of seventeen and forty dress up as a slutty nurse, slutty devil, slutty policewoman, or slutty librarian? It's an absolute shame. Oh, but what a treat it is on the first of November, All Hallows' Day, to see the girls stumbling home across college campuses, still in their slutty outfits. This is the day of deepest shame because there is absolutely no denying what has just happened. During a normal Walk of Shame, well—maybe you can at least *pretend* that you would have gone out at nine in the morning in heels and a halter top. It's been known to happen. But really, no one heads to class in the morning dressed as a slutty '50s housewife, especially one whose costume has been completely crumbled and ruined by a night under a "pimp's" futon. Our advice: play it safe and go as a slutty zombie. If you look dead and shameful in the morning, your costume will only look *better*.

Happy Halloween

slutty '50s housewife

Mid-December

Oh, students. The semester draws to a close; soon, many of you will be sent back to the crappy little towns you came from, to sit at home watching *Scooby-Doo* reruns on TBS and trying to shock your parents by claiming to have gay friends. As a result, many of you will be trying to pack in as much hook-up action as you can stand before being sent into the dry spell of exile. We highly encourage this behavior. After all, you can get with as many embarrassing people as you like—everyone will be at home for a month, so they won't have the chance to gossip about it! A special warning, however, goes out to all college freshmen. Look, we know you've all got boyfriends or girlfriends back home—terrible, boring people you now feel you've totally outgrown. News flash: they feel exactly the same way about you. But you've both matured, sexually, quite a bit over the past few months, and you both have needs. Believe us, you will have hot, awkward sex, each of you surprising the other with things you'd never have been able to imagine doing just a few short months ago. Then you will have a horrible, draining fight and never talk to each other again. We suggest that you get this over with well before Christmas, because you want to be in a good emotional frame of mind for your inevitable ill-conceived New Year's hook-up.

The Search for Clues: Girl Version

Here's a question we're asked all the time: is it still a Walk of Shame if you actually *like* the guy? Well, sadly, the answer is yes. When people gossip about this tomorrow, they're still going to say they saw you crawling home in a halter top at nine in the morning—not that they saw you crawling home in a halter top at nine in the morning *but you looked happy*.

Still, you'll feel better about the whole thing if you can summon up any affection whatsoever for the guy in question. Which leads to another problem: the typical Walk of Shame is conceived in such a terrible drunken state that you might have trouble remembering the details. Sure, you remember some vague stuff about how he looked—male, not grotesquely obese, possibly had a penis or something—but what was he *like*? What did he say to you that got you back to his place?

Was any of it true? You may never be able to answer any of these questions. And that, my friends, is why it's so important to spend a few morning moments on what we call The Search for Clues.

So listen up, Little-Black-Pantsy Drew. As soon as you wake up, it's time to get to work. Scan your environment: almost every item you find around you will help you to understand what sort of person you've just hooked up with. And to help you sort through all of that information, we've developed some rough guidelines.

The Baseline

Shallow as it may be, looks are probably the best starting point to evaluating your hook-up's potential. Also, they tend to be the easiest part to remember. So let's start there: rate your hook-up's looks on the traditional scale of one to ten. Be honest. Subtract for boils. Probably you should subtract a point from whatever you come up with even after that, because we all know how you tend to flatter yourself. Now multiply your rating by ten. This is your Search for Clues baseline. Write it down in this box: ☐

Ready to start adjusting?

Sleeping Arrangements

This one's simple: what are you sleeping on? If you're not sure, try standing up and taking a few steps away from it. If doing this means you've just fallen six feet onto a hard tile floor, then you were probably on top of a bunk bed: subtract five points. Other possibilities: bottom bunk (-3 points), single bed in two-bed dorm (-2 points; less lame, but that roommate was *totally* watching), single bed in single dorm room (-2 points; if he's good-looking, he only got a single for sex purposes; if he's not, he has no friends), couch in dorm common area (-10 points, and shame on you), futon in frat house (-6 points), twin bed in frat house (no points), couch in frat house (forget points; press charges). Better possibilities: twin bed (+2 points) or queen-sized bed (+4 points) in apartment. Subtract two points if the room, instead of a door, has a bead or fabric curtain. Subtract forty if the bed has posters or a canopy; this means your boyfriend is gay.

Make adjustments to your baseline score in this box:

The Floor

Can you see the floor? That's a good sign: add two points. Is it hardwood? Sweet: add four. If you can't see the floor, then what's covering it? If it's your clothes, how did you ever get picked up with that many layers on in the first place? If it's his clothes, subtract two points, plus an additional point for every wadded-up gym sock within reach of the bed itself. If it's pornographic videotapes, subtract or add points at your discretion, depending on how you feel about that. Another thing to look for is condom wrappers. If you don't see any, add a point: this is a man with discretion. If you see just one, that's pretty standard: no points. If you see two or three, congratulate yourself, and add three points. If you see any more than five, subtract ten points, and tell the guy his friends owe you money.

Make adjustments in this box: ☐

The Walls

Just about every guy has something on his walls, with the possible exception of pretentious architecture students. Scanning the walls is an excellent way to get to know the person whose child and/or venereal disease you may now be carrying. The images with which he has chosen to surround himself are very nearly a window into his soul. If you are in college, eighty percent of the souls around you will have elected to surround themselves with posters relating to

Quentin Tarantino films: if this is the case with your hook-up, subtract three points. If it's that poster of Belushi in *Animal House* that everyone has, subtract four. If the posters have anything to do with *Aqua Teen Hunger Force*, look deep inside yourself: do you *really* like geeks, or do you just say that to seem cool? Add or subtract as you see fit. As for well-known pieces of high art, we offer the following scale:

Dalí	-10	(he is lame)
Escher	-8	(he is lame and reads sci-fi)
Leonardo da Vinci	-6	(he is unimaginative)
Matisse	-6	(unless he's an opium addict)
van Gogh	-3	(his girlfriend bought him that)
Kandinsky	-2	(ditto)
Mondrian	0	
Picasso	0	
Bauhaus/Surrealist journals +1		(at least he's trying)
Rembrandt	+1	(he's thinking for himself)
Anything from the '80s	+4	(except Keith Haring)
Anything pre-Renaissance	+6	(he's a keeper)
El Cid	+7	(he's marriage material)
Rothko	+8	(he's too perfect to live)
O'Keeffe	+9	(he will go down on you like crazy)

If you happen to have woken up in an apartment, there's a chance the art on the walls will have been made by the guy himself, or more frequently by a friend or roommate. This is a tricky situation. You don't want the art to suck, obviously. But you don't want it to be *too* good, either, or else he'll just wind up ditching you for some hot Croatian girl who makes sculptures.

Another thing to watch out for is the guy who's covered his walls with loads and loads of pictures of his friends—fishing, mooning one another, going to formals, things like that. The last thing you want is to hook up with one of those guys who have a whole circle of homoerotic man-crush buddies. It's scary, but there really are straight guys out there who are more comfortable getting drunk and exposing themselves to one another than touching and/or talking to an actual woman.

If his walls are covered with postcards and photographs from magazines, subtract eight points. If it's comic book art, subtract two points, unless it's Wonder Woman, in which case add five. If it's nudie pictures of girls, subtract two points, unless they're clearly meant to be ironic, in which case subtract ten.

Make adjustments in this box: ⬚

Books and Music

Examining someone's collection of books and music is an excellent way to find out what they're really like. "But wait," you ask, "doesn't everyone have their own taste? Isn't it kind of subjective?" Well, yes, but here's the trick: not everyone has their own taste. Below are some handy clues that will help you figure out whether the person you've just gotten with has any personality whatsoever.

First of all, how many albums does this person own? Look around. If all you can find is a stack of twelve CDs, sitting on a desk somewhere—and one of them appears to be Bob Marley's *Legend*—you're in deep, deep trouble: subtract twelve points. What you're looking for is the same thing every guy is looking for: a decent-sized rack. He should own at least fifty CDs, and no more than five of them should be two-disc greatest hits collections. If there's a crate of vinyl nearby, go ahead and add five points—unless he wears goggles and a beret and talks with a fake English accent. DJs are absolutely terrible in bed; they keep pulling out and going over to put on a new album.

You may also want to sneak a look at the stereo and check what he was playing last night to drown out the sounds of his own grunting. A good thing to find, obviously, is music you like, or at least haven't heard of. Bad things to find include Michael Jackson's *Thriller*, Rod Stewart, or the soundtrack from *Rocky IV.* [1]

Books are even more important. Does he own any? Are they all computer science textbooks, or *Dummies* books? Subtract twenty points. You want to find at least ten books in the bedroom itself, even if there's a bookshelf in the common room. You want at least half of them to be novels; people who only read non-fiction, it turns out, tend to be really, really dull, and are always telling you way more than you ever needed to know about Grover Cleveland or the origins of the war in Chechnya. You also want to be sure that the novels in question aren't just readings for class—look for used-textbook stickers on the spine.

As for the novels themselves, what does he appear to spend his time with? You need to think hard about what sort of person you are, what sort of person you want to be around. Here's a handy guide to some of the crap kids usually read, and the questions each one raises.

---

[1] The funny part is that this isn't even a joke. Jay used to live in a dorm room next door to this guy who was supposedly Joe DiMaggio's nephew or grand-nephew or something. Whenever his girlfriend came over, he'd put on a *Rocky* soundtrack and they'd go at it. Now, even with all the disgusting things you can find on the Internet, humping someone while listening to "Eye of the Tiger" remains the sickest and most disturbing sexual practice we can think of. And no, we don't feel guilty for revealing this information: we hope the younger Mr. DiMaggio reads this, and we hope he regrets the horrible things he's done.

Ayn Rand: (-80 points) Was your worldview absolutely changed by taking that Introduction to Economics course?

Anne Rice: (-30 points; -15 if it's one of her pseudonymous S&M books) Do you like it rough? Do you fantasize about knowing how to play the cello? Do you spend most of your time in a computer lab?

Kerouac, Ginsberg, or Burroughs: (-20 points) Has your mind developed at all since you turned fourteen? Also, does he *really* have access to decent drugs?

Any other Beats: (-25 points) Is it better for a guy to read the Beats because (a) it seems like a cool thing to do, or (b) because he *actually likes* the stuff?

Robert Anton Wilson: (-10 points) Is it 1986? Do you enjoy *Doonesbury*?

Tom Robbins: (-8 points) Are you okay with a guy who will spend his entire college career wearing Cosby sweaters and wondering why hippie girls don't think he's cute?

Douglas Coupland: (-6 points) Would you date a sixteen-year-old?

Brett Easton Ellis: (-4 points) Do you want to date a film major? Is it okay if all he ever talks about is Sam Peckinpah?

Lorrie Moore: (-3 points) Are you cool with dating a really kind, terrific guy who will write you in six years to ask for your support during his upcoming sex change?

Albert Camus: (-2 points) Do you need to bum a cigarette?

Gabriel García Márquez: (-1 point) How much do you really enjoy talking about your feelings?

David Foster Wallace: (0 points) How much coffee can you drink in one sitting?

Thomas Pynchon: (+1 point) Is it okay if he annoys the hell out of you now, but turns out to be pretty okay once he turns twenty-five?

Samuel Beckett: (+2 points) Is it okay if he likes to do fake accents?

Graham Greene: (+3 points) Is it okay if he kind of thinks he's fifty?

Anything in translation that wouldn't normally be assigned in a comp lit seminar: (+5 points) Is it okay if he leaves you for a Japanese girl?

Donald Barthelme: (+8 points) Do you absolutely *need* him to make sense all the time?

Truman Capote: (+10 points) Do you mind if all your friends are convinced he's gay?

Make your adjustments in this box: ☐

The Bathroom

Don't ever leave a guy's house without making a quick stop in the bathroom. First of all, you nasty. You could totally afford to wipe up a little. Second of all, this is the absolute best place to search for clues.

But wait, you say: what if my hook-up lives in a dorm? What if he doesn't *have* a bathroom of his own? The answer to your question is: subtract ten points. There is no greater shame than reapplying your makeup in the bathroom of an all-male dorm wing.

If he *does* have a bathroom, the first thing to look into is the medicine cabinet. One medication you should know about is Valtrex, which is for the treatment of herpes. If you find any, subtract at least fifty points. And look carefully, especially if you've been picked up by a professional athlete. Also watch out for creams and ointments. Creams and ointments suggest that there is something wrong with his skin, which you've been touching all night. If there is a cream or an ointment in there, you might want to steal some for yourself, just in case.

Also check out the toothbrush and toothpaste situation. His toothbrush should not appear to have been in action for any longer than six months. It should also not have any electronic components. He should not own a WaterPik. If he fails on any of these counts, subtract ten points. While you're examining, count the number of toothbrushes, and compare with the number of bedrooms you passed on your way here. An extra toothbrush, in good condition, may indicate that he has a girl- and/or boyfriend. Same goes if the toilet seat is down. If there is any sort of art whatsoever in the bathroom, and a woman doesn't live in the house, then he is either in a serious relationship or totally gay. Subtract thirty points.

Observe also the frilliness and/or scentedness of his bath products. Any sort of fruit-based lotion and/or bath wash is a bit of a bad sign; subtract two points. An overabundance of colognes or body sprays indicates that he bathes approximately once a month; subtract five points. If he owns Vaseline, ask yourself: why would anyone own Vaseline? Subtract six points, and if you went down on him you might want to think about washing your mouth out with soap.

Make your adjustments in this box: [   ]

His Final Score

It's time to tally up!

0–30: Skeez

You should be ashamed of yourself. Now is the time to take comfort in what we discussed earlier, the Walk of Shame Personality Multiplication Syndrome, or WoS-PMS. Remember: it wasn't you who did this—it was your slutty alter ego, Danica. Tell yourself that, over and over, until you almost start to believe it. Now go on living your life as if it's true. If your friends ask where you were last night, tell them you appear to have passed out in a flowerbed. If he calls, pretend you don't know who he is. If you see him in public, pretend you don't know who he is. If he has *pictures* of the whole thing, pretend you don't know who he is. This never happened, do you hear me? This book will self-destruct in fifteen seconds.

30–50: Eh

It depends, really. How good looking are you? Do people think you're interesting? Be honest. A 30–50 guy isn't much of a find; walk down any dorm hallway and you'll find at least three of them sitting with their doors open and a Beastie Boys album on the stereo. But listen, honey: maybe that's just where you're at, you know? The good news is that this puts you in a fine, fine position. This kind of guy is usually happy to have gotten with any woman at all, and the truth is that he's never touched the same woman more than once. Except for his high school girlfriend, who is now banging the entire basketball team at a major midwestern state university. You can do whatever you want to him, and he'll stick with you— go down on him every other weekend and he'll happily buy you beer all through the in-between.

50–70: Decent

He's reasonably good-looking, there's nothing *obviously* wrong with his personality. Congratulations! Who knows, maybe he's even more interesting than his room indicates. Walk home with your head held reasonably high. Just don't get *too* full of yourself. Think about it: he's just some dull, normal guy, right? There's only one advantage to being a dull, normal guy: you can go out any night and pick up some dull, normal girl. It doesn't even matter who she is, because neither of you has any personality anyway. Watch out for the dull, normal guy. He just might blow you off next week for some interchangeably normal girl with slightly larger breasts.

70–90: Score

You're feeling pretty good, right? He's cute, and interesting—but not so cute or interesting that he won't need to call you back. Everything is perfect. Which means there's only one last test to run. Walk proudly home in the morning, and let yourself be seen. Stop and talk to people. When they ask you where you spent last night, tell them the absolute truth. Then watch their faces carefully. If they all look shocked, then he has a girlfriend. If they all look bitter, then he's an asshole. If they all smile knowingly, then he's a whore.

90+: Ultimate Score

Sounds like you've found yourself a keeper: a very good-looking guy with good taste, good hygiene, and a decent amount of discretion. So why in the world would he hook up with *you*? He could pick up much more desirable women, couldn't he? Maybe he already has a girlfriend. Maybe he has horrible taste in women because he's secretly gay. Maybe he was just doing a favor for his fat, ugly friend, and as soon as you turned out the light he slipped out of the room and sent the other guy in. Maybe he videotaped the whole thing and sold it on the Internet. There are so many opportunities for self-doubt. Our advice is to give in to them, and come up with as many reasons as you can to hate him: it's not like he's going to call you, anyway. Just go home and cry and try not to develop an eating disorder.

The Search for Clues: Boy Version

The usual stereotype is that boys are logical, rational thinkers, whereas girls are guided more by emotion and intuition. In no situation does this sound more like bullshit than when talking about the Search for Clues. Girls, it turns out, need to know things about the guy in question: what is he like? What does he do with his time? What kind of *person* is he? Guys, on the other hand, tend to have a reliable gut instinct, one that tells them exactly how to feel. All they have to do is ask their guts (and/or penises) the following questions:

1. Was she hot?	(Yes)	(No)
2. Was she annoying?	(Yes)	(No)
3. But was she hot?	(Yes)	(No)
4. Will my friends make fun of me for getting on her?	(Yes)	(No)
5. But was she hot?	(Yes)	(No)
6. Will I call her back?		(No)

Typical U.S. Walks of Shame—by State

Alabama: Can't decide whether second cousins really "count."

Alaska: Wishes there were more women around; thinks drive back from caribou reserve is a total bitch.

Arizona: Pays; returns to apartment; sits with gun in lap, watching door.

Arkansas: Thrilled about poor education system: girl really believed that Cracker Jack prize was a genuine fireman's badge!

California: Under the impression she now has speaking role in *Carnal Instinct 3*.

Colorado: Thanks lord for job as ski instructor, drunk college girls.

Connecticut: Takes train back from city to parents' mansion;

storms up to bedroom, slams door; cranks up new
Interpol album and screams at mother to bring
up a cheese plate.

Delaware: Wanders along, wondering what
smells like crab.

Florida: Withers under incredulous stares
from women in shuffleboard area.

Georgia: Drives home with sense
of immense well-being; considers
buying new rims and neon detailing
for Hyundai.

Hawaii: Is relieved to learn that state age of consent is
only fourteen; has plane to catch.

Idaho: Returns
sheepishly to militia,
hoping that he didn't mention
anything about what's going to happen on
the 18th.

Illinois: Puts hair in ponytail; drives silently home
in Volkswagen Jetta; consumes gin and Balance Bars
until last night seems like distant memory.

Indiana: Is pretty sure Jesus wouldn't have done that.

Iowa: Worries new goth look is giving people the wrong impression.

Kansas: Depressed by routine one-night stands; fantasizes about living in big, exciting city, like Lawrence.

Kentucky: Staggers slowly home, trying to remember which side of Civil War state was on.

Louisiana: Vomits; removes beads from private areas; searches city for old man with video camera from last night.

Maine: Swims back to shore, wondering how fisherman can call when there's no phone on the boat.

Maryland: Drives home, fully intending to move to a state with enough personality for humor writers to joke about it.

Massachusetts: Begins to suspect that Jamal was not actually a Kennedy.

Michigan: Stops to ask for directions back to campus; listens with dawning fear to gas station manager's accent; wonders how the hell she wound up on Upper Peninsula.

Minnesota: Wonders, briefly, what it would be like to sleep with someone who wasn't so damn blond.

Mississippi: Is distracted by nearby Civil War reenactment; enjoys part where Lee takes New Hampshire.

Missouri: Reports late for work at veterinary clinic; vows never again to cross border into East St. Louis.

Montana: Awkwardly asks if she can make a sandwich before getting back in car; has four-hour drive ahead.

Nebraska: Tries sneaking through corn to avoid detection; is attacked by rabid gopher.

Nevada: Sobers up; seeks annulment.

New Hampshire: Wonders why she can't stop falling for those tourists and their posh, sophisticated Massachusetts accents.

New Jersey: Can't be seen in public like this, hair only two meters wide.

New Mexico: Sublimates shame in terrible painting of desert landscape/flower that looks curiously like poonannie.

New York: Strides confidently down Fifth Avenue in semen-stained Prada.

North Carolina: Stops for six-course pulled-pork breakfast.

North Dakota: Shivers; counts on one hand; has now slept with every available man in state.

Ohio: Blames stripper, government.

Oklahoma: Blames Texas.

Oregon: Runs into ex while picking up soy milk at vegan market.

Pennsylvania: Stumbles over pile of horseflop; curses Amish.

Rhode Island: Gets dressed; reassures Buddy Cianci she won't go to the press.

South Carolina: Swoons, faints; wonders what happened to other half of cashmere twinset; asks mother for glass of iced tea.

South Dakota: Hitches ride to other side of reservation with patronizing college student.

Tennessee: Is now convinced she has three-album contract, with Mutt Lange to produce.

Texas: Enjoyed last night; wishes you the best on your upcoming execution.

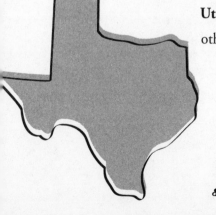

Utah: Walks down hallway to other bedroom; greets other wife.

Vermont: Gets poked awake by Phish roadies; hitches ride back to campus with fellow tasteless losers.

Virginia: Tests new memory-removal device on call girl; returns to Pentagon.

Washington: Looks over shoulder at camera; strolls casually back into forest; can't believe he had sex with human woman.

West Virginia: Retreats to opposite ends of coal mine; sits awkwardly, hoping to be rescued soon.

Wisconsin: Tries without success to get excess cheese curds out of bra.

Wyoming: Begins to suspect that bull wasn't "mechanical."

Dear Robin and Jay,

I've been in college for six whole months now, and I still haven't gotten any action. It really sucks. Every morning I see hot people taking the Walk of Shame—but what about me? When will it be my turn?

—Sexless in South Bend

Dear Sexless,

Don't fret, good buddy: your time is now! After all, there's no rule saying you have to actually hook up with anyone to take a nice, public Walk of Shame. We suggest the classic

Fake-Walk maneuver, a trick that did wonders for Jay back during his freshman year.

Next Friday night, go out to the best party that'll let you in. It may not be much—it may even be ten party dorks drinking Smirnoff Ice in a dorm—but you have to work with what you've got. Scope the place out for a while, then put your plan into motion: spend your evening talking, visibly, with the cutest girls there. Now, after a few hours of getting mocked and ignored by them, you might feel like heading home. But now is not the time for weakness. Hang in there. Don't leave until you see *them* leaving—and when they do, slip right out behind them. Then go home.

At this point, you'll want nothing more than to just jerk off and cry yourself to sleep, like you do every Friday night. But there's important work to be done. First, throw all of your clothes on the floor, and step on them a little; if you have any alcohol, spill a bit on your pants. Second, set your alarm clock for seven in the morning. Everything ready? *Now* you can jerk off and cry yourself to sleep.

When morning comes, drag yourself straight out of bed—and put on exactly what you were wearing last night. Do not, under any circumstances, bathe, brush your teeth, or comb your hair. Just throw those clothes right on and head outside. It's obvious from your letter that you've spent plenty of time peeking out your window and watching hot-girl Walks of Shame, and probably playing with yourself while you're at it; you should know how this whole thing is supposed to work. Head straight to campus and let everyone see you taking your first "Walk of Shame."

The result? Two birds, one stone. First of all, you'll have gained some valuable Walk of Shame experience—which, if all goes well, will come in awfully handy when you finally get to second base. Second, you'll have sent an important message to everyone around you: yes, yes, someone really *will* get on you. "Wait"—everyone will say—"didn't I see him at that party, talking to that one cute girl? Didn't he kind of walk out right behind her?" Well, yes, yes you did—not the best news for her reputation, but a damn good improvement for yours.

If this little scam works, you can expect at least one or two barrel-bottom drunken skanks to at least *consider* letting you touch them. From there on, you're on your own—we're writers, not pimps.

How to . . .
Make a Mask

One bag
Scissors, nail clippers, or fingernails
Marker (optional)

1. Produce bag. You may use either paper or plastic, unless you are under twelve years old, in which case (a) you should use paper, and (b) what the hell are you doing reading this book? What did we already tell you? If you can't seem to find a bag, try looking under the kitchen sink. If you can't find one there, either, two excellent substitutes are pantyhose and an extra-large condom. Although if there are extra-large condoms around, why are you going home, anyway?

2. Use scissors, nail clippers, or fingernails to poke eye-holes in bag. Before you do this, however, hold the bag to your

face, and make sure the eye-holes will actually match up with where your eyes are. You will not believe how many people get hit by cars because of skipping this very important step.

3. For an elegant touch, use the marker to draw a face on the bag. Don't worry if you can't draw very well. You look like shit, it's bound to be an improvement.

4. Place bag over head and walk, shamefully, home.

Note: In the event that you are really, really, *really* ugly, the person you had sex with may already have done this work for you.

The Rules

As world-renowned experts on the Walk of Shame, we quite frequently find ourselves wrapped up in debates about what precisely constitutes genuine Shame. It's a somewhat tricky topic. In the end, many of us in the Walk of Shame community come to the same conclusion that the Supreme Court once reached with regard to pornography: it's hard to define, but you know it when you see it. This is why Supreme Court justices have been required, since 1972, to spend at least ten hours a week watching pornography and then taking comprehension tests about the plots.

In this spirit, we'd like to take a moment to answer five of the most commonly asked questions about the rules and regulations of the true Walk of Shame.

During what times of day can a Walk of Shame take place?

The commonly agreed-upon Walk of Shame window extends from seven am to twelve noon. The reasons for this are, we hope, fairly obvious. If you can get home before seven, those who see you on the street will most likely assume that you've just had a wonderful night out partying—because really, if you were getting some, why wouldn't you stick around and keep at it until the sun came up? Thus it is that the skankiest Walk of Shamers of all—i.e., those who get their kicks and then head home without even catching a few hours of sleep in their hook-up's arms—wind up skimming lightly home, free from any shame whatsoever.

As for the noon deadline, this is a bit of a trick standard. Sure, waiting until after noon will probably keep the other people on the street from interpreting what you're doing as a Walk of Shame. But that's not necessarily a good thing. If you're out and traveling during the Walk of Shame window, people will understand: everyone's taken the Walk of Shame at some point or another, and while they may giggle and make fun of you, they'll at least be working under the assumption that you don't *always* look like that. Wait until after noon, though, and this is no longer a morning Walk:

this is who you *are* now. Some people, in fact, may conclude that you're actually just going out for the day—that you deliberately left the house looking like a zombified slut, and will be returning home the next morning looking even worse.

It must be noted, of course, that these time considerations are highly flexible, depending both on your location and the activities in which you are taking part. Many scholarly volumes, for instance, have been written on the Walk of Shame in Alaska and through the polar latitudes. Nobody knows what the hell's going on with the sun up there. Sometimes it's shining at night, sometimes it's dark for a month, sometimes you talk to a guy for thirty minutes at a party before realizing he's a moose; all the confusion makes it awfully hard to figure out who should look ashamed and who shouldn't.

Is it still a Walk of Shame if you like the person?

Yes. This whole liking-the-person business is one of the worst Walk of Shame rationalizations we've ever heard. First of all, as mentioned elsewhere in this book, the other people on the street don't know whether or not you like the guy: all they know is that you look kind of trampy and have your skirt on backward. If you're willing to walk all the way home carrying a sign that says "I REALLY LIKE THE GUY WHO DID THIS TO ME," then fine—you're off the hook. Your peers won't think you're taking the Walk of Shame—they'll think you're a drugged-up performance artist. Otherwise, honey, just give it up and face your shame.

Second, and more importantly: does it really matter if *you* like the person? The core of the "but I liked him" rationalization, so far as we can tell, is that you're trying to pretend that you and this person didn't just get it on, but rather that you began some sort of meaningful relationship, thereby exempting you from the usual Walk of Shame rules. After all, you like him, and last night he seemed to indicate that he liked you. He will totally call, right, and you'll totally start dating, and then everything will be fine.

Do we even need to dignify this with a response?

So being in an actual relationship exempts you from the Walk of Shame?

Under limited circumstances, yes. To begin with, if you're honestly engaged in a genuine relationship, then you probably won't look particularly Walk of Shamey in the morning: you'll have remembered, we hope, to bring along a comb and a toothbrush, and the person you're involved with will hopefully let you use their shower. Perhaps you'll even have brought along a change of clothes. Better yet, if you're a girl, you'll have the opportunity to borrow some of *his* clothes, and take the exact inverse of the Walk of Shame—the Walk of I Have a Boyfriend. You will stroll happily home wearing the tiny No Fear T-shirt he's been hanging onto since middle school, and everyone will know that you're in love.

Situations remain, however, in which even couples can wind up—quite by accident—taking a Walk of Shame. First, we come to situations in which the couple, for whatever reasons, have declined to make their relationship public. These couples will be cursed to take some of the most dangerous Walks of Shame ever: if you don't believe me, *you* try explaining to your sister what you were doing readjusting your bra in front of her boyfriend's apartment. Second, we come to the problem of couples who live close to each other. In situations like this, it's common for them to meet up spontaneously, safe in the knowledge that they can spend the night together and then easily slip home to fix up before the day begins. This is a kind of safety you shouldn't count on. Everyone will see you taking what looks very much like a Walk of Shame, except now there will be an added element of embarrassment: hey, everyone will think, doesn't that guy already have a girlfriend? Even tougher are situations in which both members of the couple live in the same apartment building or dorm, giving everyone around them intimate knowledge of the duration, frequency, and noise level of their trysts.

Does there have to be actual sex involved for it to be a Walk of Shame?

We were hoping to answer this question with a point/counterpoint debate between former president Bill Clinton and Ken Starr, but Clinton wouldn't return our calls. The first issue is how we choose to define sex. Now, if you're under the age of fifty, not involved with any evangelical Christian groups, and don't know what "heterocentrism" means, you'll probably define sex as involving the penetration of the vagina with the penis. Also the anus, though most people who aren't total whores start with the vagina and work their way up. Except for gay men, in which case, sure, the anus. And lesbians. It's hard to draw any clear lines about that stuff, and I'm not about to try. If in doubt, just videotape the whole thing and start an Internet poll.

Now, if actual sex of this variety has occurred, you

certainly qualify for a Walk of Shame. The same goes for oral sex. Actually, the same goes double for oral sex, which is for some reason kind of the stock and trade of collegiate hook-ups. And not mutually satisfying two-way oral sex, either. Honestly, if you're a guy, and in college, and you happen to be reading this, we have some advice: go down on people. Seriously. It will make you really, really popular. Sometimes it seems like guys have to turn twenty before they figure out that they're allowed to use their mouths.

Basically, you're good to go if any two of the six following things have taken place: (1) orgasm of either party, (2) penis exposed and handled, (3) vagina fingered/"oil checked," (4) underwear fully removed, (5) nipples regularly manipulated with tongue over period of at least thirty minutes, (6) either party tied up, otherwise restrained, and/or spanked. If you somehow *haven't* managed to get past second base, then chances are you're a total priss who will walk home feeling completely ashamed and paranoid that everyone is looking at you and knows exactly what you've done, despite the fact that you look completely normal and boring and everyone is ignoring you as usual.

I travel a lot for business. Is it still a Walk of Shame if you do it in a place where nobody knows you?

It depends on two factors. First: has your family been in America for a while? If so, you're probably okay. If not, you might want to worry. One of the amazing things about immigrant mothers is that they have been able to create intricate networks of observation and gossip, allowing them to achieve something the government likes to call Total Information Awareness. So you go to a conference in Houston, and wind up going back to your hotel room with some guy from the London office, and as soon as you get home, ring ring: turns out your mother's third cousin goes to church with a woman whose daughter-in-law was working the desk when you bought all those Trojans at the gift shop.

Beyond that, it kind of just depends on where you are. Walks of Shame don't count quite as much, for instance, in Las Vegas, Jamaica, South Beach, Cancún, and—weirdly—Duluth.

Your Sense of Direction: A Quiz

Making your way through a Walk of Shame will require you to exhibit complete poise, concentration, and navigational ability. Is *your* sense of direction up to the task? Try this quiz—and find out whether you have what it takes to move confidently and efficiently in the direction of home.

---

1. It is nine a.m. You are facing the sun. Which direction are you facing?

a. North

b. South

c. East

d. West

---

2. You leave your TA's apartment and walk north for one block. You then turn right, turn left, and turn left again. Which direction are you facing now?

a. North

b. South

c. East

d. West

3. You are walking along near the Robert Taylor Homes, on Chicago's South Side. You see a sign reading 47th Street. After proceeding in the same direction for one full block, you see another sign reading 48th Street. You are:

a. Walking south

b. Walking north

c. About to get mugged

d. A and C

4. You leave a lovely woman's apartment and ask a passerby for directions. You are instructed to walk home via Peachtree Lane, Peachtree Street, and Peachtree Avenue. Which of the following names does *not* describe the U.S. city in which you live?

a. Hotlanta

b. Fort Worth

c. ATL

d. Gonorrheaville

5. According to your friendly neighborhood pirate, your current bearing is at a 30 degree angle to the North Star. Unfortunately, after walking 3.84 miles in this direction, you remember that your friendly neighborhood pirate's sextant is always off, by a margin of plus or minus 18 degrees. How much distance could this error have added to your journey home?

a. What is a sextant?

b. I don't know any pirates.

c. 1.26 miles

d. None of the above

6. You have just woken up in a twin bed in a dank basement, with a pentagram of *Magic: The Gathering* cards taped to the ceiling and the cheek of an acne-scarred thirty-four-year-old nestled against your shoulder. After vomiting, you run upstairs and meet your new friend's parents, who express delight that their son has finally acquired a "little girlfriend." Assuming you can run at a constant speed of 10 miles per hour, how long will you need to run before you will feel comfortable stopping?

a. Five minutes

b. Seventeen minutes

c. Two hours

d. Until Andy Rooney finally does us all a favor and drops dead

7. After traveling for a few short minutes, your new girlfriend's husband removes you from the trunk and begins pouring concrete over your feet. You are currently blindfolded, but you can hear the sounds of water moving around you. You are:

a. In Brooklyn, facing north

b. In Jersey, facing east

c. In Odessa, Ukraine

d. B or C

8. As you stumble through the blinding white force of the blizzard, you can barely make out a blurry figure that appears to be that of a polar bear. Moments later, you stumble across a small squeaking animal that appears to be a penguin. You have:

a. Started losing your mind

b. Wound up at the North Pole

c. Wound up at the South Pole

d. Once again violated clearly posted zoo rules

9. After a blissful weekend with CyberLordSavage, the dominant S&M enthusiast you were lucky enough to meet via the Internet, you find yourself commanded to make your trip home while wearing a curious device—an inflatable buttplug with a compass attachment that directs it to increase significantly in size whenever you are headed due north. CyberLordSavage resides in San Diego, California, and you, CringingMaiden81, currently reside in Indianapolis. You should arrange to switch flights in:

a. Denver

b. Portland, Santa Fe, Missoula, Oklahoma City, Minneapolis, and Little Rock

c. Santa Fe

d. Dallas

10. Your intern wipes her chin, offers you another slice of pizza, and leaves the office. To return to the residential wing of your house, you will want to walk:

a. North

b. South

c. East

d. West

Answers

1. c. East

2. d. West

3. d. A and C

4. b. Fort Worth

5. b. I don't know any pirates

6. d. Until Andy Rooney finally does us all a favor and drops dead

7. d. B or C

8. a. Started losing your mind

9. b. Portland, Santa Fe, Missoula, Oklahoma City, Minneapolis, and Little Rock

10. c. East

Your Score

1–3. Are you okay? Are you blond? We recommend that you abstain from sex entirely until you can at least figure out how to open a carton of milk. If you leave a guy's house with a sense of direction like this, there's a very serious chance that you—assuming you don't first get hit by a bus or wander into the La Brea Tar Pits—will walk in a great big stupid circle, and wind up strolling right back into his apartment exactly one week later, looking even sluttier than last time.

3–6. You just might make it home, but you definitely need to work on your navigational skills. Buy a map, take it home, and just practice folding and unfolding it. This process stimulates the alpha waves of the brain, making you ever so slightly smarter and more creative: do it for a few years, and you just might eventually be able to read the map itself.

6–9. Heh heh: six to nine. Congratulations. You have a well-developed sense of direction, one that will help you make your way home even when your Walks of Shame lead you to confusing or frightening locales. Some girls have to rely on cab drivers to recognize their addresses. But you, missy, you can walk out in public with your head held high, confident that you more or less know how to get back to your own place of residence. Wait, wait: why are we congratulating you for this?

10. Excellent work. Not only do you have a keenly developed sense of spatial relationships, but you also understand the intricate play of power and submission at the core of every Internet S&M relationship. Give yourself a hand. Now let us ask you something: have you ever considered using your talents to help others? Next time you're taking a Walk of Shame, look around and you'll notice countless confused-looking girls, standing underneath streetsigns and counting on their fingers, or standing in the rain and asking strangers which way the sun is. Have a heart: give these girls the help they so dearly need. If they look more jacked-up than you, there's a good chance they'll also serve as cover.

Fashion Tips for Your Walk of Shame

Conventional wisdom has it that no one looks good during a Walk of Shame. Your hair is snarly. Your clothes are sweaty and slept in, or else crumply from hanging over some guy's guitar stand. You've got day-old makeup smears and hideously fresh hickeys. None of it stands a chance of being attractive, right? That's the conventional wisdom. But look at it this way: What has conventional wisdom ever done for *you*? If you had any of this "conventional wisdom," you would have kept your thong on last night.

Besides, think back: some of you might remember a moment in the mid-'90s when the fashion world went nuts over this thing called "heroin chic." The idea was that it would be sexy to watch very skinny, dirty-looking models stumble around looking angstful and homeless. And it turned out that a whole lot of people thought it really *was* hot. Even now, there are people in this country who think Vincent Gallo is hot. People in this country and in France.

So then consider this: for your average heroin addict/ Vincent Gallo, *every waking moment* is a Walk of Shame. Sometimes you can't even tell the difference. Jay, for instance, lived across from a methadone clinic for three months before he realized the ragged-looking hipsters wandering around every morning weren't just taking a Walk. Then for two months he was positive they were film students, until two of them stole his car stereo.

The point is, we figure the Walk of Shame look is totally ripe for a high-fashion makeover. And after many hours (two) of looking through *Glamour* (me) and *Teen People* (Jay), we've come up with some tips on how to pull it off.

Fall Fashion (Ladies)

The fall look should be one of girlish innocence. Lots of curiosity, with just the hint of a naughty streak underneath. It helps to really get into the part. Pretend you just came to college from a small town in Indiana. You've never really done much with guys, but you're secretly excited about maybe getting in on a wet T-shirt contest at some point. Or going down on someone in the library. Maybe even another girl, you know, behind some stacks in the main library at Vassar. Really let yourself get into it. Dance around your bedroom singing along to Michelle Branch CDs and fantasizing about professional basketball players. Then try out these stylish looks.

- *ponytail*
- *no makeup*
- *inappropriate top*
- *tight jeans*

The Ponytail

It's sporty and casual. For true girl-next-door appeal, you want to mount the ponytail as high on your head as possible. Nothing says Adorable Little Skank-in-Progress like a nice bouncy topknot. Plus it makes guys think about oral sex. If you got that joke, you're not playing the part right yet.

No Makeup

Give yourself a good scrub before you leave his place, for that fresh-faced glow. Sure, you won't actually be glowing, and may in fact look a little ill. Don't worry: guys rarely notice what's going on with your face.

Inappropriate Top

This Walk of Shame basic can add just the right dash of sex appeal to your fall look. Slender ladies should try a halter; bustier gals will do fine with an ultra-tight T-shirt. Fall mornings get chilly, and a little "oops, how embarrassing" peek-a-boo from the nipples can give you that mischievous appeal you're looking for.

Tight Jeans

They're pretty much the only way to go. Notice the beer stain on the leg of this number: it's the perfect touch for letting everyone know what a fun, flirty, down-to-earth girl you'll be until approximately December 12th.

Fall Fashion (Gents)

Guys: the fall look is about boyish, All-American sweetness. Take it from a woman who understands. There's nothing more adorable than watching some little man walk home with a big puppydog grin on his face, all because he just barely managed to feel up some actual breasts for the first time since prom. It melts the heart—it's like watching a baby learning to walk. And we cherish these moments, because we know how time flies: soon enough, he'll be acting all distant and sulky because his girlfriend won't give in on the whole anal sex thing.

Bedhead

Chances are that you, like every other college boy on the planet, were already sporting some kind of ill-advised bedhead look even before you went out last night. Re-creating it *without* the half-pound of hair gel will give you valuable practice for when you're out of school and totally broke.

Hickey

The hickey is a classic fall look for men. Just try to look cute and sheepish about it. Remember: it's a hickey, not a signed affidavit that you had a threesome with the Olsen twins.

Inside-out T-Shirt

It's cute, it's casual, and it hides that lame "vintage"/ "distressed" Abercrombie & Fitch bullshit on the front.

Jeans

This is another no-brainer—you've been wearing them since July anyway. If you want to have any decent winter Walks of Shame, you'll have to learn that hanging them over a fan and blasting them with Febreze is *not* the same thing as washing them.

Winter Fashion (Ladies)

Ladies, winter has come, and hopefully you have, too. These days you know exactly what you're doing, and you want a sophisticated look to match. You're a girl who knows her way around. You have your pick of the best guys. You're confident and proud. These are the bald-faced lies your winter look should tell everyone around you.

DONT WALK

- *bedhead*
- *hickey*
- *inside-out t-shirt*
- *jeans*

115

Greasy Hair

Down and dirty is the way to go. This season is all about that shameless nature-skank look. Plus guys don't really understand the difference between dirty as in dirty and dirty as in *dirty*.

Perfect Makeup

See if you can't get it in shape before you bolt. Sporting perfect night-out makeup early in the morning doesn't just let everyone know where you've been—it makes you look like a total professional about it, too. A Walk of Shame retouch is the female equivalent of that guy who's always got empty condom wrappers lying around on his desk.

- *greasy hair*
- *perfect makeup*
- *whiskerburn*
- *little "I got laid" dress*
- *heels*

Whiskerburn

Don't cover this part up. Some shiny red whiskerburn lets everyone know what you've been doing, and assures all passing authorities that you did it with someone old enough to shave.

Outfit

Here's where you really need to embrace the Shame. A little dress—or, better yet, a formal dress—is always good, the ultimate in "I got laid" visibility. But think about it: who *doesn't* get laid on a night like that? Try a simpler look. Pair those tired black sorority-girl stretch pants with one of those low-cut sorority-girl peasant blouses. Now you look like you went out in 1997 and still haven't made your way home yet.

Heels

The early-morning stiletto-heel stagger is a true Walk of Shame classic: if you can walk straight, you're not really doing this right. You should look like you could go horizontal at any moment, just like last night.

Winter Fashion (Gents)

Hey, guys: it's winter now, and you've been around the block. The only people on the block turned out to be a chick from the marching band and a chubby girl with a third nipple, but no one else needs to know that. From here on out, you're taking your Walk in style. Once again, professionalism is the key word: try and pretend you know what you're doing. We all know you don't, but it's just polite to pretend.

Wet Hair

Just splash some water on it. It'll either leave you looking slick and sleazy, or like some girl enjoyed your company enough to let you use her shower. Nobody cares if your head freezes, you big pussy.

Tired Look

This is critical. There is nothing less sexy than a guy who looks like he had sex and still found time for a good night's sleep. Everyone at that party saw you put five hours of flirting and hounding into taking that girl home—do you really want them to know the encounter itself only lasted four minutes? You're a man, not a commercial break: *look tired.*

- *wet hair*
- *tired look*
- *inside-out sweater*
- *shoulder bag*
- *stolen socks*

Inside-out Sweater

It makes you look hurried and mussed, and just might keep you from wearing that awful blazer with the elbow patches that you think looks so suave and professorial.

Shoulder Bag

This is one of those subtle tricks that scores big points. It's one thing to look like you went out for the evening and scored. But add a bag, and you look like you can't even walk from your room to the library without getting laid along the way.

Stolen Socks

One of the biggest morning-after benefits to a good hook-up is nicking a clean pair of socks from her dresser. Remember: you've been wearing yours for five days, and she's only worn hers for six hours. When you're putting your shoes on in the morning, just slip into the wrong pair.

Spring Fashion (Ladies)

Spring has always been about fashion flair—playful, carefree styles full of vibrant color and youthful chic. Have fun and experiment. By this time, everyone knows who it is you've hooked up with anyway. Why not take it to the next level? Take a page from the extravagant glamour of the Italian runways, and step out looking truly skanktastic.

Lubricant in Hair

Looks almost like gel, but adds more volume. Just avoid—and you've really got to take my word for this, because I don't want to get into it—just avoid the kind that heats up when you touch it.

Ruined Makeup

It's the ultimate Walk of Shame look: smeared-out eyeshadow, runny mascara, off-center lipstick. You want to wind up somewhere between Courtney Love, a mid-'80s Cure fan, and a PBS Kabuki special. Worried you might get picked up for prostitution on your way home? That just means you need a little more lipstick on your teeth.

Tank Top

A tank top spells it out: you don't need to dress up to get action. You just throw on some laundry, walk down toward the liquor store, and see what happens.

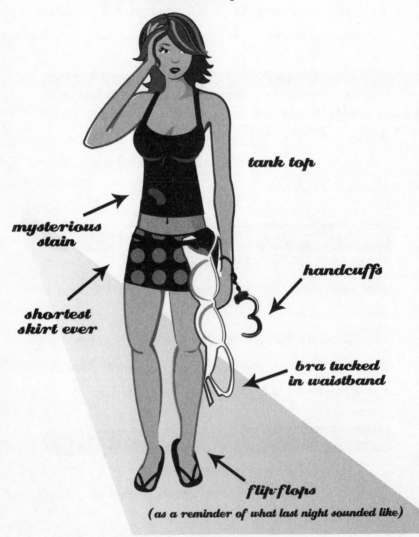

lubricant in hair
& ruined makeup

tank top

mysterious
stain

handcuffs

shortest
skirt ever

bra tucked
in waistband

flip-flops

(as a reminder of what last night sounded like)

Bra Tucked in Waistband

Bonus points if you honestly look like you don't know it's there.

Handcuffs

The spring look is all about fantasy. I refuse to accept that you don't have at least one fantasy that involves handcuffs.

Various Mysterious Stains

I don't even want to know what that stuff is. On the other hand, Jay does, and so will every guy you pass.

Shortest Skirt Ever

A good Walk of Shame skirt is short enough to make you really, really wish you knew where your panties ended up. For women who live near beaches, substitute any pair of shorts that wouldn't look out of place in a Nelly video.

Footwear

This is a tough choice. Boots are always good. Not Uggs, or fashion cowboy boots, or junior-executive "I carry an umbrella" boots—ridiculous falling-over boots, maybe even over the knee. Alternatively, there are also flip-flops. The constant slapping noise will (a) draw attention your way, plus (b) provide a sweet reminder of what it sounded like last night.

Spring Fashion (Gents)

I had sex last night?

Letter to Jay . . .

Dear Robin and Jay,

I was raised in a very strict, proper household. When I
came to college, everyone made fun of me for my conservative
ways. Now I'm ready to loosen up and maybe take a couple
Walks of Shame. But it all seems a bit sudden. I can't just go
from an innocent girl to a raging slut overnight, can I?

—Tentative in Tennessee

Dear Tentative,

This is a question we get asked all the time, and there are
two answers. The first answer is the literal answer. Can you go

from an innocent girl to a raging slut overnight? Sure you can. Jay will even help. You didn't include a number.

As for the figurative sense, well, we understand your dilemma. What you need is a guide, a role model to show you how to make that delicate transition from a sheltered little girl to a skanky, sticky woman. Now, when it comes to sexual guidance, we're pretty sure there's only one place to look— and that's the Disney Corporation. Some of popular culture's finest little-girl/slut conversions have been executed by former Disney employees. Consider, just as an example, a little thing we like to call the Lindsay Lohan Principle.

Check it out: as of 1998, little Linsday Lohan was starring in Disney's updated remake of *The Parent Trap*. Wasn't she sweet? Adorable, freckled, overacting . . . it just warmed the heart. A scant six years later, and . . . holy shit, she's practically Tara Reid. How did this happen?

For Lindsay, it was all a matter of the slow fade. And don't think for a second that the slow fade came naturally—she worked at this transition. The whole thing was nearly ruined, in fact, when she woke up at sixteen with sudden, massive knockers: the only way she could keep things on track was to try to make people feel guilty for checking out a sixteen-year-old's rack. (Oh, but Lindsay, dear, how could we *not*? Those things are totally gonzo.) The masterstroke was getting that little guy from *That '70s Show* to pretend to be her boyfriend.

The result? Without our ever *really* noticing, Miss Lohan went from child star to drunken big-haired titzoid miniskirted Paris Hilton wannabe.

So listen, Tentative: take her cue. Start out simple. The next time you go out drinking, take a purse with you; before you leave the guy's house in the morning, give yourself a good retouch. The time after that, not so much. Take it slow. Give it a whole year's worth of slow fade. If you can get to winter break having people still think you're a sheltered little girl, you're doing great: by summer you'll be stumbling around naked and people will think it's so adorable how you've come out of your shell.

• *Neil Bush* •

Profiles in Shame: Neil Bush

*P*residential siblings . . . always an embarrassment, aren't they? Many of our readers will likely remember Roger Clinton, an on-and-off addict in a truly horrifying rock band. Looking back through history, we find even more humiliating examples. Millicent Eisenhower was indicted for tax fraud. Richard P. Hoover was suspected of Satanism. James McKinley was so addicted to cocaine that he lost the ability to sneeze, and died after being served a dish of pepper steak. Apart from Robert Kennedy, the only notable presidential sibling we can conjure up much sympathy for is Theodore Taft, who was devoured by his twin brother, William Howard, while still in the womb.

Our Hall of Shame honors, however, must be offered to the first and best shameful presidential sibling of the 21st century: Neil Bush. The competition for most shameful Bush offspring is actually quite a tight one, as anyone familiar with the life works of Neil, Jeb, Marvin, and Norbert is surely well aware. But Neil's story is without question the finest.

Skipping over Neil's involvement in a number of 1980s savings and loan scandals, we come to his fateful trip to Thailand, during which he . . . yes . . . wait for it . . . okay: had sex with Thai prostitutes. Well, everyone makes mistakes, right? Neil's real blunder, though, was to try and skirt those mistakes with an excuse *so* lame—so incredibly ridiculous— that it'll make even your most absurd Walk of Shame lies seem like the Gettysburg Address. According to Neil Bush, well, he arrived at a hotel room . . . and walked in . . . and there were some women there . . . and they had sex. Happens to everyone, right? Sometimes you just walk into a room, and there are a bunch of Thai women inside, and you totally bang them. At least now we know who's been writing all of those "I never thought it would happen to me" letters to *Penthouse*.

When asked if he thought the whole thing might be a little, you know, *strange*, Neil was ready once again with the perfect response: "It was very unusual."

Neil Bush: for sticking to your guns and telling the absolute worst Walk of Shame–related lie ever given voice by modern man, we salute you. Welcome to our Hall of Shame.

Homeless or Walk of Shame?

Can you tell the difference between a homeless person and an extreme Walk of Shamer? Take this quiz and find out.

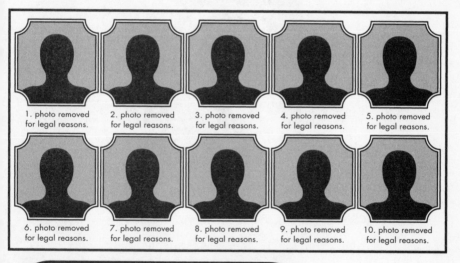

1. photo removed for legal reasons.
2. photo removed for legal reasons.
3. photo removed for legal reasons.
4. photo removed for legal reasons.
5. photo removed for legal reasons.
6. photo removed for legal reasons.
7. photo removed for legal reasons.
8. photo removed for legal reasons.
9. photo removed for legal reasons.
10. photo removed for legal reasons.

Answers

1. Homeless
2. Homeless
3. Walk of Shame
4. Homeless
5. Walk of Shame
6. Walk of Shame
7. Homeless Walk of Shame
8. Walk of Shame
9. Homeless
10. Courtney Love

How to . . .
Pretend to Be Deaf

A business card

A pen

Your keys

An incredible insensitivity toward the genuinely disabled

1. Note, below, the American Sign Language symbol for "I am deaf." Practice these movements until you can execute them swiftly and confidently.

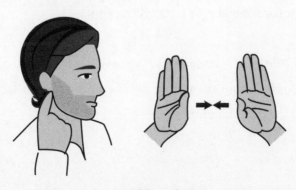

2. Before leaving your place of shame, turn over the business card. Use the pen to write the following on the reverse, blank side: "I am deaf. $2.00."

3. Remove your keys from their keychain.

4. If anyone you know tries to talk to you during your Walk of Shame, use your knowledge of English Sign Language to communicate that you are deaf.

5. If anyone you know seems baffled by your use of English Sign Language, place your keychain in their hands, and show them the back of the business card. Wait approximately ten seconds, then snatch the keychain back and walk casually away.

6. If anyone tries to communicate with you in English Sign Language, begin to cry. Then run.

Note: It's essential to remove your keys from the keychain before attempting this. Someone may, in fact, give you the two dollars.

Your Drink
of Choice

*I*magine you're about to experience a Walk of Shame. You've just awoken in some strange boy's apartment, mostly undressed, head throbbing. Oh dear, you think—how did *this* wind up happening? Who'd have imagined things were heading down this path?

The truth is, anyone could have guessed. You may not have noticed, but there's a direct correlation between what you were doing last night and where you've ended up this morning: who you were with, how you were dressed—and, most importantly, what you were drinking.

Yes, your beverage of choice. Both Jay and I have done extensive research on this topic—starting at the age of approximately fifteen—and we've discovered a direct connection between various sorts of liquor and the types of shame they lead to. Based on this information, we're prepared to offer a rough guide to your Walk of Shame experience.

1. Beer

Oh beer, glorious beer! Beer is the cornerstone and staple of most collegiate Walks of Shame. But as any fool knows, not all beers are created equal. We've separated them into a few major categories. First, you have beers like Coors, Natural Light, Rheingold, and El Presidente, all comprising a category we like to refer to as "Crap." These beers, with their watery, overcarbonated tastelessness, will lead you straight toward the least classy Walk of Shame possible: you will wind up being groped on a dirty couch by a sports enthusiast who tries to "finger" your bellybutton as the two of you belch continually into each other's mouths. A slightly better category of low-cost beer is the one often referred to as "Watery Domestic," which

 despite the title may include Canadian beers as well: here we find Rolling Rock, Icehouse, Goose Island, Samuel Adams, and similar. These beers are your best bet for a comfortable, normal Walk of Shame, the kind that doesn't involve puking or bondage gear. The last category of low-cost North American beers is the one we call

"Chic," including such hipster favorites as Old Style and Pabst Blue Ribbon. Drink these beers and you will spend the next two weeks suffering through terrible shows by some guy's terrible garage-rock band.

The next important category: standard imports, including such beers as Beck's, Heineken, Amstel, Corona—even ritzier imports like Hoegaarden and Oberweis. The only problem with drinking beers like this is that you will wind up with partners who think you're actually serious about seeing them; they will call you and call you and expect the two of you to go out together on actual dates that involve talking and spending money. This is the last thing you want. It only gets worse as you move along into the fifth category, which encompasses most imported beers more expensive or classy than Guinness—particularly fruity things from Belgium, things that come in weird foot-high glasses, and things from Africa or east Asia. Drink these beers and we promise you: you will wind up in a weird little book-filled apartment with someone who works for a non-profit advocacy group.

2. Wine

If you're a college student, wine might seem a tad "adult" for your purposes. In fact, it's the ideal drink for you. First of all, it's cheap: a jug of delicious Gallo Rhine rarely costs more than ten dollars. Second of all, it'll leave you with a much more manageable hangover than many of the alternatives. Third, it will lead you to have joyous group sex with a bunch of comparative literature majors while someone prances around you in a circle, declaiming selections from "Howl." If you're in grad school, wine's power is even more pronounced: you will finally get with that guy everyone in your program thinks is totally hot but totally gay.

3. Cocktails

Whether at the bar or at a house party, cocktails are always an excellent choice. Of course, there are countless different types of cocktails, and you must choose your beverage with great care. The cardinal rule here is not to drink any frilly floofy "girly"-type drinks. There are two good reasons for this, neither of which has to do with your being a total pussy (though that's a pretty good third one). The first is that there is absolutely no worse hangover than the one that involves periodically puking up maraschino syrup. The second is that girly-drinks send the worst of all possible signals to the men around you—i.e., "I have never been drunk before and will, shortly, be very vulnerable"—

resulting in come-ons from the worst possible men. In most cases these will be men who absolutely cannot for the life of them get laid, and so have switched into that terrible predatory mode where they think they can *trick* somebody into sleeping with them. As soon as they see a round of Umbrella Sours hitting your table, they'll close in with a whole list of pick-up lines they remember from a book they read when they were twelve years old. This is absolutely not the kind of man you want your child support payments to be coming from.

If you're going to drink cocktails, go with something classy. As far as we can tell, there's nothing quite so beautiful as a crisp gin and tonic with a slice of lime. Cocktails to avoid include rum and coke (you will take your top off in public) and screwdrivers (you will puke like a banshee and it will be *orange*). Also, when drinking appletinis, you should check all men's hands for wedding-band tans.

4. Shots

Nothing will send you hurtling toward a genuinely shameful Walk of Shame quite like a series of straight, gut-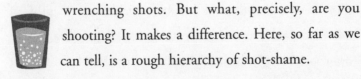wrenching shots. But what, precisely, are you shooting? It makes a difference. Here, so far as we can tell, is a rough hierarchy of shot-shame.

Shame Level A = Vodka Concoctions. Including lemon drops and the like. These are pretty tame, shot-wise, and will probably only get you as far as making out with some loser in the hallway to the bar restrooms. Get through enough of them, though, and you just might surprise him by taking him home, rubbing yourself all over him, and promptly passing out.

Shame Level B = Tequila. Watch yourself, girl. Tequila won't just lead you into a Walk of Shame—it'll have you doing things in public that everyone involved will want to forget. Doing tequila shots will lead you to urinate in strange places, expose yourself to priests, take bets on how many fingers you can get in your mouth at once, and a whole lot of other things you'll regret tomorrow. The good news is that the actual Walk of Shame bit kind of pales compared with everything that preceded it. The bad news is that you will totally sleep with whoever was standing nearest to you at the end of the night, and it will probably be one of your friends.

Shame Level C = Goldschläger. If you've never experienced this cinnamon-flavored filth, be aware that it's a horrible, spicy spirit, with flakes of "genuine" gold floating in every bottle. It will lead you to the absolute depths of depravity. And worst of all, you will wake up tomorrow to take a nauseating hungover dump, and you will learn that all of that "genuine" gold has turned your shit green. That's not a joke: if you don't believe us, we highly encourage you to do seven or eight shots and see for yourself.

Shame Level D = Ultimate Shame = Jägermeister. Granted, Jäger is a wonderful thing. If nothing else, the experience of a good Jäger drunk, with its weirdo psychological effect, is certainly "interesting." Unfortunately, when it comes to hooking up, it's not the kind of "interesting" you necessarily want. Strange things will happen. You will start having an odd conversation about S&M with some homely girl from your dorm, and wind up tying her up in the laundry room. You will run into someone you absolutely loathe and wind up having rough "revenge" sex. You will spend your entire student loan payment on prostitutes. And the results will be very "interesting."

Obviously there are a great many drinks we haven't covered here. But if you've been paying attention, you should be able to figure out what we'd say about the drinks listed in the following quiz. Which of these drinks will lead to worthwhile Walks of Shame?

1. Banana daiquiri?

2. Straight whiskey?

3. Mike's Hard Lemonade?

4. Sparks?

5. Zima?

6. Everclear/Grain alcohol?

7. Pimm's Cup?

Answers

1. No. See girl-drink rule, above.

2. No. You will sleep with someone with lots and lots of tattoos.

3. No. Remember: the last thing you want is for your puke to taste fruity.

4. Yes. This stuff is a godsend, and the caffeine just might keep you alert enough to use good judgment.

5. No. Girl-drink rule + sugary-puke rule + getting-picked-up-by-effeminate-guy-in-turtleneck rule.

6. Yes. The walk isn't as shameful if you seriously have no idea what the hell you did last night, or last week, or ever, or who you even are.

7. Yes, although you may wake up on a yacht, which makes the "walk" part more difficult.

Excuses for Your Walk of Shame— by College Major

Anthropology: Learned in Human Sexuality class that chances of actually getting HIV are sort of exaggerated.

Art History: Mother sent you to college to find a husband; by god, you'll do whatever it takes to make her proud.

Biology: Had something to do with one of those glands they keep talking about.

Business/Marketing: Soul already black as night, so why not?

Chemistry: Using self to test proposed "Season-After" pill.

Classics: Lecture on Caligula got everyone all hot.

Communications: Got confused; happens a lot.

Comparative Literature: It was the only way you could get boys to argue with you about Sartre.

Economics: Detected demand, provided supply; guy said he was Milton Friedman's grandson.

Education: Trying to report for grade-school teaching-assistant duty feeling slightly less horny.

Engineering: Built giant steam-powered bong; can't remember what happened after that.

English: Just emulating Henry Miller.

Film: Working on biting, satirical spoof of porn industry; digital video will back this up.

Fine or Visual Art: It was on the syllabus.

Foreign Language: Catalan men "so sexy"; only men on planet who will chase after chubby, homely blondes.

History: Bored; horribly, suicidally bored.

Journalism: Hard-hitting interview with student government candidate escalated into shouting match, ended in passionate kiss.

Liberal Arts / General Education: Couldn't decide who to sleep with; decided to just sleep with lots of different people as a compromise.

Mathematics: Everyone in your major sleeps with one another in a desperate attempt to convince themselves that they are not socially retarded, acne-ridden dorks.

Music: Vibrations from cello kept running up thigh, stirring unexpected emotions.

Philosophy: Not sure on what epistemological basis one can claim actual first-order sex was actually had.

Physical Education: $80,000 athletic scholarship does not require going to class or work; not sure how else to kill time.

Political Science: Practicing cover-ups for post-election gay sex.

Pre-Med: Stocking up on orgasms in preparation for med school dry spell.

Psychology: What's really fascinating is how transparently *your* interest in other people's sex lives reveals your subconscious feelings of rejection and aloneness.

Religion: Conservatives' worst nightmares have come true: study of non-Christian religions has led to complete moral relativism. Just kidding. The guy was hot.

Sociology: Conducting intense fieldwork concerning sexual mores of North Americans.

Theater: Just wanted another chance to make lots of noise and have someone look at you.

Women's Studies: Trying to get back into the good graces of popular lesbians.

Famous Walks of Shame

As discussed throughout this volume, the Walk of Shame is a commonplace topic in the worlds of film, literature, and music. We offer this convenient guide to some of history's most famous Walks of Shame in the hope that it will prove both entertaining and educational, or at least fill up enough space so that we can finish writing this and get paid. Note that all of the information that appears on the following pages—and indeed, through the entirety of this book—is completely factual and true.

1. "Billy Jean" (song)

The Walk of Shame themes in this popular song are quite clear, and many of them are made even more transparent in the accompanying video. In this classic piece of cinema, we see Michael Jackson making his way home, early in the morning, before sunrise. His paranoia is so strong that he imagines the squares of the sidewalk are lighting up beneath him, calling attention to his presence and the shameful things he has just done. The song's lyrics indicate a state of deep denial: "Billy Jean is not my lover," he says, trying desperately to convince everyone around him that he is merely out for an early-morning stroll. But look at his pants: clearly he's been forced to borrow a pair of trousers from his paramour, as they are much, much too short for him.

In order to understand the true Walk of Shame subtext in this song, however, one must have some idea of the convoluted history of its production. Records reveal that when Jackson first submitted the track to his record company, the title was actually "Billy Smith"—the name of the "kid" mentioned in the chorus. (When Jackson sings "the kid is not my son," he is in fact defending himself not only against accusations of child molestation, but of incest as well.) The executives at the label quite naturally felt that this subject matter was far too delicate for a pop song, and instructed Jackson to rewrite the lyrics so that it was about knocking someone up instead. Thus was the public briefly fooled into thinking that Michael Jackson had any interest whatsoever in sexual intercourse with adult women.

2. *The Iliad* (epic poem)

This classic of Western literature is essentially the story of the greatest, bloodiest, and most dramatic Walk of Shame in all of human history, and we have only ranked it after the "Billy Jean" video because there are no panthers involved. No matter what Hollywood producers or classics professors may try to tell you, the plot of *The Iliad* boils down to this: Helen, the most attractive woman in Greece, meets Paris, a Trojan man. They drink a great deal of ouzo, and following a steamy make-out session, Helen—displaying an almost collegiate lapse of judgment—decides to go back to Troy and move in with Paris, which incidentally is totally a girl's name. This angers the Greeks, who pretty much already thought the Trojans were total dicks. They conscript their finest warriors and sail off to Troy, where they begin a war that lasts for years and years. Many, many people are killed. Finally, someone mentions an idea he's had about a giant wooden horse, and the other Greeks slap him with pieces of leather and ask why he couldn't have mentioned that two or three years back. In the end, after slaughtering all of the Trojans, burning their city, and enslaving their women, the Greeks recover Helen, who sits somewhat awkwardly through the boat ride home.

3. *Rocky* (film)

Okay, you remember that part of the training montage where Rocky is jogging and his coach is bicycling behind him, shouting encouragement? Maybe it's just us, but we've always gotten kind of a homoerotic sense about that shot. We're not sure exactly what it is—maybe all of the raw-egg swallowing that bookends it—but the sexual tension there is almost as thick as between Jay Leno and that guy who leads his band. We get the distinct sense that the night before they must have slipped a little past the boundaries of the boxer/coach relationship, causing a certain awkwardness between them.

4. "American Pie" (song)

We are often told that this song is about the plane crash that took the lives of Buddy Holly, Ritchie Valens, and the Big Bopper, and that Don McLean's sneering references to Bob Dylan ("the Jester") and Mick Jagger ("Jack Flash") represent a criticism of the contemporary music scene. This is probably true, but it misses the deeper point of "American Pie": this song is obviously about having sex with overweight prostitutes. For one thing, it has the word "pie" in the title. For another thing, research has demonstrated that the song is just long enough to listen to once through during the drive to McLean's North Carolina home from a certain brothel outside Reno, Nevada.

Misty Lomano, the proprietor of said brothel, says she remembers the precise day McLean came to visit, and offers the following account: "He came in with about three thousand dollars—a lot of money, in those days—and asked if we had any 'large women.' Those were the words he used, 'large women.' So I sent him up with a girl we had then, a girl named Beulah, kind of a porker. Well, an hour later he comes back down, and says she wasn't big enough. Well, I says to him, I suppose there's always Lucy, but we don't get much call for her anymore—she's up over two hundred pounds these days. But he seems to like the idea. So I set him up with Lucy. But an hour later he's back again—still not enough for him. Sheesh, I say, well, how about this—there's a girl I know, Big Dottie, used to work here, she's been on disability the last few years, she's gotta be at least four hundred pounds, can't hardly get out of the house at all. Well, let me tell you, he sure liked the sound of that. So I called her up and said three grand, what do you think? And lickety-split, she buzzed her motorized scooter right up over to the place. He stayed up there with her almost till morning, having the time of his life.

Eventually I had to come banging at the door, and I says to him, I says, Listen, you've used up your three grand's worth, time to head home. He comes out looking kind of sheepish, he says to me, How about I play you a song? I'll play you the most beautiful song you ever heard for just another hour with that gal. Well, you don't run a business like that, that's what I think. So I said no dice, time's up. Listen, buster, the levee's dry. Well, you should have seen the look on that man's face. He looked me right in the eye, he did, and he says to me, If me and my guitar and my songs aren't worth another few minutes with that beautiful gal, then music's dead to me. Be that as it may, I says to him, it's time to go home. So he goes right on out to his Chevy, looking awfully hangdog. I'm going to write a song about this, he says. And I promise you right here, it'll make me enough money to spend a whole month with that gal. Sure, I said, whatever you say. But what do you know, that's exactly what he did. And let me tell you, if Dottie hadn't died of a stroke that year, I reckon he would have married her."

5. *Madame Bovary* (book)

One of the wonderful things about *Madame Bovary* is the psychological precision with which Gustave Flaubert portrays his subjects. Another is the fact that the title character is a total vapid skank. It's very hot. If you haven't read this book, it's basically the story of a woman named Emma who blows all of her husband's money on clothes and then starts bumping uglies with another guy in the back of a horse-drawn carriage. It's where they got the idea for *Sex and the City.* Anyway, in those days you weren't allowed to describe actual sex in a novel, not even if you were French, and so the only way you can really tell when Emma gets laid is that the carriage goes in circles for an hour, and then afterward there are some strange Walk of Shame moments. It's a great work of literature, and we totally recommend it.

6. *Cast Away* (film)

Okay, think about it. Tom Hanks is on the island for like *years*, right? And his only companion is a blood-encrusted volleyball named Wilson. There is a lot of time on the island that we don't actually get to see, which is probably a good thing, because the movie is still about an hour too long. But this we do know: by the time Hanks builds his raft, he is seriously, seriously in love with Wilson. Now, say all you want about the need for companionship and support, but let's face it, men have needs. No one in the world is ever going to convince me that Tom Hanks didn't try to hump that volleyball, not at least once.

7. *Star Trek* (television program)

The original series of *Star Trek* is to be commended for presenting its plots with the utmost moral seriousness, and for offering a vision of the future built on the most laudable, egalitarian ideals of Western culture. Still, it was basically a story about a guy who couldn't stop boning aliens. Planet after planet, he sailed on through the cosmos, scoring with chicks whose genitalia may or may not have been traditionally compatible with his own. Much of the story's weight comes from anticipating the moment that Captain Kirk would look deep within himself, recognize the emptiness and futility of his one-night extraterrestrial dalliances, and come to terms with the obvious: the true love of his life was and always would be that guy in the red shirt who got shot on the "Western" planet.

8. The Bible (book)

One of a few cool things about the Old Testament is that it's chock-full of Walks of Shame, some of them *really* sleazy. I highly recommend checking it out: if you skip over the who-begat-whom and don't-eat-this-animal parts, you get pretty much nothing but nudity, murder, gay sex, and human sacrifice. Of all the Walks of Shame included in there, our personal favorite is the tragic tale of Samson. Samson was a guy who made a deal with God that if he never cut his hair, he would have extraordinary strength, making him pretty much the hottest guy ever. And in true bad-boy fashion, he went around kicking ass in the interest of justice, making him pretty much the world's first superhero. Then he met this woman named Delilah, who genuinely did dig him—there weren't a lot of long-haired hardbodies back then, so he was a total catch—but was also being pressured by various authorities to sell him out. So one night, she got him really drunk, made out with him for a while, and then got him to tell her about the whole hair thing. Then, when he passed out, she cut off his hair and handed him over. This story has all the makings of a really terrific, tragic Morning After. Just remember this the next time you're stumbling home across campus: at least you didn't castrate God's chosen hero or lose all your superhuman powers to some girl with a few bottles of wine and a nice rack.

Afterward, Samson is forced to push a millstone for the rest of his life. But then they drag him out to mock him at some big public ceremony, and God gives him the strength to tear the building down on everyone's heads, thereby making him the world's first ultra-religious terrorist.

9. *The Phantom of the Opera* (book, musical)

There's only one thing worse than falling in love with a horrible acid-scarred freak who lives in a basement, and that's the music of Andrew Lloyd Webber. The guy is basically a gayer, more pompous Elton John, except without the good '70s material to look fondly back on.

10. *Oedipus Rex* (play)

In the final slot, we come to the king of all Walks of Shame, a Walk of Shame an entire lifetime in the making. It is a story of royalty, riddles, murder, incest, and old men with tits. (Tiresias: seriously, look it up.) When a king learns a prophecy that his own son will kill him, he abandons the newborn child in the wilderness, assuming—in much the same fashion as a James Bond villain—that everything will go according to plan, and nobody will be all like "Aww, a baby, we'd better rescue it." But the child *is* rescued, and eventually returns to the city. After saving the place from a terrible curse by answering a Sphinx's riddle, he kills the king (his father), and gets down to porking the holy hell out of the queen (his mother). Eventually, when he learns the truth, he is so ashamed and shattered that he puts out his own eyes, and spends the rest of his life wandering blindly around Greece with only his daughter, Antigone, to keep him from tripping over things and falling into the Aegean. It would have made more sense to us if he'd just cut off his own dick, but you don't second-guess the masters.

The moral of the story is this: Don't fuck your mother.

How to . . . Make Your Own Toothpaste

Altoids, Tic Tacs, Smints, Certs, or any other commercial breath freshener
Your underwear

1. Place eight to ten breath-freshening mints in your mouth. You may experience a slight pain in your salivary glands. Wait two minutes, without swallowing.

2. Wrap the gusset of your underwear around your index finger.

3. Just before your mouth begins to foam uncontrollably, use your index finger to rub along all sides of your teeth.

4. If your underwear happens to be a thong, you may also wish to floss.

mrs.
federline

· Britney Spears ·

Profiles in Shame: Britney Spears

oor, poor Britney. It's been hard for her, you know? Growing up in the spotlight, hounded by the paparazzi, tabloids leaping on her every move . . . it certainly couldn't have been easy.

One of our favorite pop culture Walk of Shame moments, in fact, came when little Britney cracked under the pressure. Picture it: a gorgeous night in Las Vegas, Nevada. People from all over the country are out and drunk and having great fun, gambling, watching shows, experiencing perfectly legal sex with state-regulated prostitutes. And our dear sweet Britney, well—if Vegas is fun for the average person, just imagine what it's like for a famous young multimillionaire with a killer ass. There's our poor little Britney, whooping it up with her friends, drinking, flirting, and . . . getting married to some guy she wasn't even dating?

Yes, all it took was one fateful night. Britney got hitched to a "childhood friend" with the unfortunate name of Jason Alexander, just like that guy who played George on *Seinfeld*. And that—horrifying as it might be to wake up in the morning and realize that everyone in the country is momentarily going to wonder why you married George from *Seinfeld*—isn't even the kicker. No, the real shame began when Britney called her mother, in Florida: "Guess what, Mom? I got married!"

Scant hours later, Britney's mom was on a plane to Nevada. Scant hours after that, she landed in Las Vegas and immediately set about getting Britney's marriage annulled. Next time you're stumbling your way across campus, just remember that a young, famous girl got married—and her fucking *mom* flew out, in full view of the public, to tell her she couldn't. It doesn't get any more mortifying than that. Unless . . . well, unless you get married again, barely a year later, to some dancer whose ex-girlfriend is about to have his baby.

Letter to Jay...

Dear Robin and Jay,

Lately I find myself taking quite a few Walks of Shame from a particular fraternity. It's probably not worth going into why. Anyway, there are three possible routes to get me home. One of them goes right past a hospital. The second takes me right past the English Department offices. (I'm an English major.) The third takes me right past a retirement home. Which one should I take?

—Lost in Lexington

Dear Lost,

You pose a couple of interesting questions. First of all, how the fuck are you an English major when you can't even spell? I swear to god, we had to correct the spelling of eleven different words in your letter, including "English."

In response to your actual question, we're kind of surprised that you've bothered to ask: all three sound like decent options. The advantage of the hospital is that hospitals are the only place where no one cares if you look crappy. For all they know, you could be sick. And have you ever taken a good look at nurses? Cruddy scrubs, bags under eyes, no makeup; they aren't exactly women who are out to look their best. Nothing wrong with a Walk of Shame via hospital, not in our book.

Under normal circumstances, the English Department wouldn't be such a great idea. But look, if you're really getting passed around an entire fraternity, chances are you look exactly as skanky as you sound. Everyone in the department knows what you're up to already, so you might as well give them a little tease by letting them see you in action. They might even come to admire you a little.

Still, after weighing the options, we've decided to recommend the retirement home route. Why? As a public service. Remember: old people may not really be "people" anymore, but they were at one point, and in many cases they still do have feelings. And there they sit, cursed to spend the rest of their days gumming stale food and watching one another have strokes. Why not give them a little dose of excitement?

Besides, shameful as it may feel to be making your skank-walk past your elders, the truth is that they're pretty much used to it. One thing people don't realize about Alzheimer's patients is that if you leave them alone together, they will totally get it on. After all, what do they care? And more important, what do they care about *you*?

Best of luck, Lost, and remember: use a dental dam.

The Absolute Worst People to Run into During Your Personal Walk of Shame

1. Your Boss

It may sound unlikely, but this has actually happened to a friend of mine, a woman we'll call "Tracy." She will vouch for me: your boss is the number one absolute worst of the absolute worst people you could possibly run into during a Walk of Shame—particularly if you already suck at your job as much as Tracy did. Here's the problem: now, every time you fall asleep in a meeting, or forget to file an essential memo, it's not just because you're lazy or incompetent like everyone else around you. No, no—now it's because you're too much of a whore to do your job properly.

Silver lining: None, unless you're angling for a spot as the boss's "personal assistant"/sex toy.

2. Neighborhood Homeless Folks

No disrespect is intended toward the homeless. There are plenty of homeless people in my neighborhood who are lovely to have around, and I am more than happy to stop and chat and provide them with cigarettes. But nobody really wants homeless guys all up in their business. Especially the pricky variety, the ones who are always acting hurt and betrayed when you tell them you don't have any spare change: believe me, once one of these guys catches you knock-kneed and bedraggled in an eight a.m. miniskirt, he *will* be all over you for weeks and weeks, giving you knowing looks and talking at you like *he* was the one you went down on in the bus on the way back from the formal. Or whatever it was that you personally did.

Silver lining: Some men may be too busy making sex jokes to remember to ask for your money.

3. Your Gynecologist

This is another situation that may seem unlikely, but once again I have direct confirmation, from a girl we'll call "Monica." Even worse, in Monica's case it was (a) a man, (b) a man she'd seen not even two weeks prior, and (c) a man who for some reason pronounced the procedure "Pap schmear," as if there might be cream cheese involved. Male gynecologists, you must understand, are a problem, and not simply because they're male; the problem is that they're usually nervous and polite about being male, so they wind up talking far too much and overexplaining things, waving instruments in your face and saying dumb obvious things like "Okay, now I'm going to put this inside you." They tend to sound remarkably like those guys who—contrary to all evidence—have decided that their cocks are incredibly huge, and say things like "Is that okay? I'm not hurting you, am I?" This was the sort of gynecologist Monica was cursed to have, which doubled her mortification when she stepped out onto a local sidewalk and found him strolling along with a newspaper tucked under his arm. And he *nodded* to her, which is simply cruel.

Silver lining: There is none. This person's relationship with your vagina should be strictly professional, and there is something just demented about his knowing that you actually *use* it.

4. Your Parents

Either of them. Why, you ask, was this not number one? Well, because—believe it or not—your parents are well aware of what you're up to. If they seem not to be, it's only because they've toned it down in their heads, to make it cute and acceptable. For instance, when I was seventeen, my father sat down with me and my boyfriend and gave us a lengthy talk about how we might be "tempted to experiment with sex." This would have been absolutely true and on-point, had he merely added the word "anal" to that sentence. This is how parents keep sane: whatever they're willing to let themselves imagine is completely laughable compared to the truth. So if you live such a strange, tiny life that there's any serious possibility of seeing either of your parents during a Walk of Shame, simply act embarrassed and tell them that you're thoroughly ashamed to have drunk *alcohol* last night, and gotten sick, and been forced to stay at a friend's apartment. They will thank you.

Silver lining: If they believe you, they may buy you breakfast or give you a ride home. I imagine this depends on what you're wearing.

5. Crotch-Sniffing Dogs

Somewhat tasteless, but it needs to be said. What could be more embarrassing than standing in a group of people and having some perverted beagle nose straight in on your crotch? Dogs are wonderful, but they have very little tact. Worse still, the dog's owner will always say the same thing—"He does that to everyone"—but this is clearly not true, and we all know what the man with the leash is thinking: he's thinking, hmm, I wonder what she's got going on down there. This is typically bad enough with periods—trade it in for Walk of Shame stickiness and I assure you, it's mortifying.

Silver lining: If your date concealed an explosive in your vagina, you're saved.

6. The Person in Question

This is why, once you're out of that dorm room or apartment, you should walk directly home. And quickly. Stop in the guy's neighborhood for breath mints or coffee, and you run the risk of stumbling out of the convenience store and straight back into the arms of the problem. This is especially dangerous if you've just (a) slipped out while he was still asleep, (b) made a big stink about how you can't believe you got drunk enough to hook up with *him*, or (c) had a threesome.

Silver lining: If it was fun, you might as well go back upstairs and start it up again. If you stay past noon, the whole walking-home bit is slightly less shameful: instead of looking skanky, you just look terrible.

7. The Police

I'm not sure why; possibly this one is personal. Possibly it's that you're already doing pretty well in terms of guilt-feelings. Possibly it's that some of them will give you that possibly-a-ho once-over, as if they're going to tail you around the corner and make sure you don't pick up an early-morning trick.

Silver lining: Are you lost?

8. Professors

The problem with professors is that they're exactly the people you're most likely to run into on a college campus at seven in the morning. They will be exceedingly chipper and morningy and pleased to see you; they may even want to discuss a paper you've recently submitted. And once they realize what you've been up to, ninety percent of them will give you odd smiles every time you see them for the rest of the semester. You will never again be able to drop in for office hours, and if you ask for an extension on any assignment whatsoever, it will be assumed that you're only behind because you've been too busy dry-humping international students. TAs, on the other hand, are a slightly different matter, insofar as they're young and occasionally quite cute. Running into certain TAs during a good Walk of Shame can actually be a great thing—they get to see you worked up in a sexual state, and you can bet that they'll spend the next few weeks trying to picture the whole thing. You will get much more individual attention in review sessions, and once the grades are out you'll receive a strange little e-mail asking you to come out for a drink and "discuss" the course.

Silver lining: Contrary to popular belief, the vast majority of professors will not actually sleep with you and then give you a better grade. I know people who aren't me who learned this the hard way. But seeing you in a state like this is as close as they'll come, and if you look good enough you may get a little bit of grade inflation.

9. Your Significant Other

This goes somewhat without saying. If you do encounter your girlfriend or boyfriend during your extra-shameful Walk of Cheating Shame, we suggest the following excuses: (1) Unexpected invitation to pimps-and-hos costume party. (2) Passed out in ditch. (3) Rushing to hospital; victim of alcohol poisoning. (4) Slipped roofies by unidentified white male. (5) Glad to see him/her; have been lost for days. (6) Last time you let mother-in-law take you shopping. (7) Suffering from amnesia. (8) "You look just like this guy my twin sister's dating." (9) Turning tricks to afford extra-special anniversary present.

Silver lining: May spare you an awkward break-up conversation.

9.5. Exes

Exes are something of a special case: it all depends on the situation. The worst kind of ex to run into during a Walk of Shame is obviously an ex who dumped you for being too drunk and/or slutty, especially if you denied it. Another bad one is the ex you dumped for someone else, someone you were sure you'd be with forever. Some other winners are the ex who was at the same party last night, and saw exactly who you left with; the ex who was way better in bed than the reject you spent last night with; and the ex who points and laughs. If you really are unfortunate enough to run into a bad ex during a Walk of Shame, the most important thing is to keep steady: don't lie or make excuses. Just casually mention that Jude Law is in town and turns out to have a *gigantic* penis.

The Absolute Best People to Run into During Your Personal Walk of Shame

1. Slutty Friends

It's a proven fact: standing next to an unattractive person makes you seem that much more attractive. The same goes for skankiness. There's nothing like a good friend, a shoulder to lean on, someone to look ten times as shameful as you and draw all the attention her way. This is why we suggest that all ladies, when going out for the evening, draw lots to select a Designated Slut. This person is required to wear something provocative, something that will look shameful and possibly illegal when seen on the street at nine the next morning. Then, pick a meet-up spot, something convenient to all nearby frat houses. When morning comes, anyone in the group who finds herself still out can adjourn to the assigned meet-up spot, and walk safely home, with the Designated Slut providing cover. It's possible, even, that people will think you're both returning from some kind of fantasy semi-lesbionic threesome scenario, which—believe us—will totally raise your cachet with the boys in the dorm.

2. Art Students/Fashionistas/ Performance Artists

Art students, like people who work in the fashion industry, are practically immune from the Walk of Shame. For art students, it's the way they dress: they're so covered over with fake "weird" affectations that you can't tell anymore what was meant to be attractive and what wasn't. As for those in the fashion industry, they're some of the few people who can stand on the street at 8 a.m. in ridiculous slutwear and reasonably claim that they're on the way to a morning meeting. If you meet members of either of these groups, just borrow an accessory and try to blend in. The same goes for performance artists, who are very often naked in public before noon.

3. Taxi Drivers

The first boon is obvious: you may now be able to travel in the backseat of your own private Shamemobile, slouched low enough to be invisible to all those on the sidewalk, enjoying the soothing sounds of conservative talk radio and/or an extended sitar jam. But wait, you ask, what about taxi-driver shame? No problem. Anyone who's ever ridden in a taxi will likely have noticed that a great number of drivers are not originally from this country. Many of them, in fact, come from countries where women do not traditionally reveal their hair, arms, ankles, or noses. As a result, these drivers may not have internalized American concepts of skankiness, making it all pretty much the same to them. They've spent years driving carloads of drunk *Sex and the City* wannabes to and from exciting gay bars, and they've pretty much seen it all. You could be having sex back there, and they'd just yell at you not to get anything on the seats.

4. That Guy Who Wears the Trenchcoat

Extensive research has proven once and for all that every single college in North America has this guy. He is disturbingly skinny and buttons his shirts all the way up and wears a trenchcoat all day, even in summer. In sixty-four percent of cases he will add a fedora to the ensemble. If you haven't seen him around, it's probably because he spends all day playing *Magic: The Gathering* at the coffeeshop and all night in the computer lab. In any case, he's an excellent person to spot. Simply walk up and ask him for his trenchcoat. Since he has never been directly addressed by a woman who wasn't legally or contractually obligated to speak to him, he will temporarily be rendered speechless and motionless. While he is frozen, remove the trenchcoat and wrap it around yourself. Just remember: this is a dangerous maneuver. If you don't get away fast enough, people may think you are out on a date with him.

5. Those Girls from Your Dorm with No Friends

You know the ones. The worst part is that it's their own desperation that dooms them to loneliness: they're so damn eager to make friends with you that they come off insanely clingy and provoke a flight response. The terrible clothes don't help. The good news is that they're very often up early in the morning, with others like them, wandering around campus singing showtunes and trying to convince everyone that they are indeed enjoying themselves. Do your best to walk past them. Say hello, if you get a chance. This will forever draw a line in the sand between you and them. Last night, you got action. Last night, they popped a big bowl of popcorn and sat home in the dorm watching *Felicity* on DVD and talking about which boys—including the one you were busy straddling—are "cute." This is the way the world is supposed to work, and they need to know that. Sure, there's a chance that they'll try to look down on you for it, to pity you as some drunken tart with no self-respect. They may even pray for you. But don't worry: deep, deep down—not even that deep, really—they are consumed by self-loathing and envy.

6. Your Bartender

Apart from your closest friends, there's only one person with whom you can really laugh about a good Walk of Shame: the bartender who got you there. They see this all the time, and they like it. They look at you, all hungover and skanky, and they feel a little glow inside, the warm, fuzzy feeling of knowing that the work they do really *does* matter. Stop and chat, because we guarantee a good bartender will make you feel much, much better about the whole situation. Also, if you're cute—free drinks!

7. Zombies

This is kind of unlikely, but some days it's worth hoping for. After all, compared to zombies, you're remarkably put together, right? There's not much difference around the face, but at least you have all your limbs. Our advice is that if there's a graveyard anywhere near your usual Walk of Shame route, drop by a library and bone up on your zombie-raising incantations. They're the best cover a girl could ask for. Just remember to retouch your makeup a little before you start raising the dead: on a particularly bad day someone might come after you with a chainsaw.

8. Anyone with Gum

Your breath reeks. Seriously, it's like a horrible combination of Jägermeister and penis. You need gum, or mints, or even garlic. So if you don't run into your local vampire-hunter on the way home, look out for anyone who might have any gum: grandmothers, junior executives, schoolchildren. Maybe not schoolchildren. Then walk right up with your hand over your mouth like a giggly Japanese girl and ask for a piece. We understand that you may be tempted to just get home as soon as possible, avoiding all human contact, ducking behind trees and pretending to be deaf. But it's worth the investment. You never know whom you might run into on your doorstep, and a fresh, minty mouth will give you the confidence you need to look them right in the eye and say you just got back from a fishing trip.

9. Coworkers

This one is ever so slightly counterintuitive, but it's absolutely true. Sure, the conversation will be awkward, but you will have established something very important: you have a life. Some of them, it turns out, may not—and again, a line needs to be drawn. Second of all, some of them will begin to admire your ability to function properly in a job setting *and* keep up with your sexual gallivanting. Third of all: again, if you are cute, you will suddenly find various guys around the office doing your work for you. Cultivate your reputation as the one person in the workplace who has been empirically demonstrated to be sexually available.

9.5. Exes

We've already established that running into certain exes can be problematic. But look at the bright side: there are plenty of exes you can be happy as hell to encounter in a state like this. This category, in fact, includes eighty percent of guys who broke up with *you*—especially if their reasons had anything to do with sex acts you declined to perform for them. With the right ex, you'll enjoy flaunting your Walk of Shame. Hike your shirt up even further, let your whiskerburn glow red in the sun, and give your mascara that extra smear, for a true over-the-top vamp-skank look. Chances are, he'll never have seen you looking anything like this: let him know it.

A Complete History
of the
Walk of Shame

About a week ago, our editor suggested that it might be fun and/or educational for this book to include a complete history of the Walk of Shame. To which we replied—and we stand by this—that what she was suggesting sounded like a lot of work, more than we were really prepared or qualified to do. After that there was a lot of arguing and tossing around of terms like "incompetence" and "breach of contract," and eventually we said okay.

Since then, we've spent a lot of time and effort researching the true roots of the Walk of Shame, including—but not limited to—watching The History Channel, looking at "vintage porn" online, using common sense, and conducting extensive interviews with this guy at our bar who says he's working on a Ph.D. in history. Not only is he an expert in the field, but he's also a terrific guy, and he picked up the tab on enough Maker's Mark to convince one of us to expose himself to some tourists. The only problem is that we don't really remember so much about the interview. But we spent the next day trying to reconstruct it from our notes, and here's basically what we came up with.

Prehistory

Here is an actual napkin on which our friend reproduced a famous Cro-Magnon cave painting found in southern France:

Mesopotamia

The phenomenon of the Walk of Shame dates all the way back to the world's first significant agricultural settlements, in early Mesopotamia. Back then, Walks of Shame were a lot longer, because people had farms, so it was a long way from one house to another. Of course, with the rise of civilization came also the rise of sexual morality, and women discovered taking a Walk of Shame were subjected to a test of their purity. They were stripped naked and tied to a post in a cow pasture. If they were touched first by a light-colored cow, that meant they'd gone "all the way" with the man in question, and would thus be crushed with large stones. If they were touched first by a dark-colored cow, that meant there was no actual penetration, and they would simply be burned, with the man involved given the opportunity to start the fire. Mercifully, women in these days were rarely caught taking the Walk of Shame, as there were no alarm clocks, and people slept late.

The Holy Land

As mentioned in previous chapters of this volume, the Old Testament is an amazing source of Walk of Shame history. One of the stories contained therein—the tale of Samson—was actually great enough to deserve a place in our top-ten list of famous examples. Other Old Testament Walks of Shame you might want to look into include the part where Adam and Eve realize they're naked; the ultra-sleazy David and Bathsheba liaison, which has some high-level political intrigue behind it; and the story of Noah's Ark, which I can't seem to read without imagining stuff happening on that boat. Shameful, shameful stuff.

Ancient Egypt

The ancient Egyptians believed, like many in modern cultures, that their pharaohs were literally gods upon the earth. One of the drawbacks of this belief was that it made it kind of hard for the pharaohs to date. In one royal bloodline, in fact, brothers and sisters were forced to intermarry for generations, in order to keep the divinity of the family untainted. Gross, right? Plus imagine how you'd feel the morning after hooking up with your creepy-looking inbred sister.

Ancient Greece

The rich history of the Walk of Shame finds its most literary moments in the Greek, or Hellenic, culture. The Greeks were highly preoccupied with the Walk of Shame, as can be seen in their myths and literature. For instance, Zeus, foremost among the Greek gods, was constantly turning into different kinds of animals and humping unsuspecting chicks. This would result in two very different Walks of Shame. Zeus would go home to Olympus and blow off his wife, Hera, who was sort of understandably a total bitch about this kind of thing. On the other hand, a whole lot of girls wound up slinking home in the morning hoping they hadn't just gotten knocked up by a bull or a swan, which in most cases they actually had.

Refer, once again, to previous chapters, for an in-depth description of history's longest-term Walk of Shame, as depicted in Homer's *Iliad*.

Ancient China

It is told that countless generations ago the emperor tired of the attacks by the Mongol hordes, who would loot Chinese villages, lay waste the land, and rape the women. It was decreed that an immense wall would be built, to forever defend his fair land from the calumny of the Mongols. Many generations later, the emperor's descendant traveled hence to see the completion of the wall—and found, on his side, a lone Mongol horseman, trotting up and down the length of the wall. "Nothing," said the horseman. "What? I mean, I was just visiting for breakfast. Is there a gate here, or anything?"

Great
Wall
of China

Ancient Rome

The wealthiest citizens of the ancient Roman Empire were incredibly prosperous and powerful. Unfortunately, they didn't have any TVs, so they spent most of their time arguing about what to invade next and dreaming up ridiculous ways of entertaining themselves: taking baths with one another, watching people get eaten by wild animals, or just gorging the fuck out of themselves on big plates of meat. Thus did the lifestyle of some ancient Romans reach mind-boggling levels of decadence, especially because back then there wasn't always some asshole around pointing out that that kind of behavior was exactly what led to the fall of the Roman Empire. In an atmosphere like that, you'd better believe the Walk of Shame was a common occurrence. For some Roman emperors, it even involved short hallways and blood relations.

The Dark Ages

After the fall of Rome, Europe was overrun by various groups of angry, marauding tribes—including the Vandals, who were angry because no one had invented spray paint, and the Goths, who were angry because no one had invented mascara. Empires crumbled, chaos reigned, and many marauding tribes galloped home razzing one another about the over-weight village women they'd ravaged during the previous day's looting.

Elizabethan England

One of literature's most romantic Walks of Shame comes in William Shakespeare's classic *Romeo and Juliet*. In Act III, Scene 5, we see the young lovers awaken in Juliet's chamber, having evidently just gotten it on hardcore. A brief argument ensues in which Juliet, being either kind of horny or kind of clingy, claims that it's not morning yet, and that it is the nightingale, and not the lark, that they hear singing. Romeo, however, knows he's got a long trip to Mantua ahead of him, and mostly just wants to get the hell out of there.

Like all great literature, the discussion that follows offers us great insight into the human condition, as well as into the conflicting emotions wrapped up in any good Walk of Shame. Romeo, when warned to be careful during his travel, optimistically shrugs off the whole thing: "All these woes shall serve," he says, "for sweet discourses in our times to come." Juliet is somewhat more pessimistic about the matter, and announces a premonition that she'll next see Romeo "as one dead in the bottom of a tomb." Then, in Shakespeare's clearest evocation of the Walk of Shame condition, she comments: "Either my eyesight fails, or thou look'st pale."

The Renaissance

The period of the Renaissance was a critical turning point in the history of Western culture. It was during these long centuries that European civilization developed many of the morays, values, and cultural ambitions that would lead it boldly into a glorious, enlightened future of taking over other continents and stealing all of their stuff. It was also during this period that Europeans began to produce larger and larger amounts of cultural artifacts, allowing us to imagine with greater precision how their lives were led.

One notable figure associated with the Renaissance is Leonardo da Vinci—painter, writer, inventor, physician, and all-around, you know, Renaissance Dude. (Back then there wasn't very much to learn about any one particular topic, so you kind of had to spread yourself around.) Leonardo's main contribution to the history of the Walk of Shame is revealed in this excerpt from one of his early notebooks:

"Returned this morning from L's house. The looks of the citizens on the street! I could scarcely bear the venom of their expressions. What to do? I have tried to put it from my mind. Spent the afternoon working on the painting of myself as a chick."

The New World

The discovery of the New World by the major seafaring powers of Europe touched off a centuries-long race to exploit the people and resources of this new territory—and a fascinating series of clashes between the people of the Old World and the indigenous people of the New. In North America, Europeans mostly just killed the natives they ran into, and only banged and/or married them in a somewhat ashamed, clandestine way. In South America, on the other hand, the Spanish intermingled with the indigenous peoples much more freely, resulting in a rich mestizo culture. Lots of Walks of Shame happened on both continents, except instead of winding up with gonorrhea or herpes the way they do nowadays, people tended to wander home with smallpox.

Colonial North America

One of the most famous of history's Walks of Shame took place at the start of the Revolutionary War. In the bustling American city of Boston, a renowned silversmith named Paul Revere took leave of his wife, Rachel, to ride over the Charles and indulge in a lengthy round of doggy-style sex with a chambermaid named Betty. Unfortunately, post-orgasm, he fell dead asleep, and so instead of sneaking back to Rachel at a reasonable hour, he was forced to ride home quite conspicuously in the dead of night. A few blocks from Betty's home, however, Revere was struck by the perfect distraction. "The British are coming!" he shouted. "The British are coming!" Luckily for Paul, the British really *were* coming, and the philandering silversmith went down in history as a genuine American hero.

Napoleonic Europe

Napoleon was very, very short. It's often theorized that this was part of why he wanted to take over Europe—you know, the whole "short man" complex—but this theory is belied by the fact that Napoleon actually had a very, very large penis, and felt more or less confident in his manhood and sexual potency. (This as opposed to Adolf Hitler, who, while several inches taller, had a scrotal abnormality that made him terrifically self-conscious and incapable of true scrotal intimacy and/or mutually satisfying teabaggery.) Toward the end of the eighteenth century, Napoleon met and married the woman with whom he is most often associated, the island-born Josephine. Unfortunately, Josephine could bear him no children, and so he divorced her, in the first legal divorce entered under the Napoleonic Code. It's funny how things have changed, isn't it? The last thing you have to worry about these days is that a guy will ditch you for *not* getting pregnant.

Victorian England

England's Victorian era is often remembered as the height of social formality in European history: a period of high moral standards, sexual repression, and overwhelming propriety. This is kind of a funny misconception, insofar as it was also the most recent era of English history in which you wouldn't be considered weird for picking up ten-year-old prostitutes. Believe you us, the Victorian period was *filthy*, full of secret buggery and child molestation and illicit congress with farm animals. And remember—back then they hadn't really invented lube yet.

But, much like American evangelicals and Congressional Republicans, the Victorians talked a good game, and all of that lip service to God and propriety successfully covered the dim, grimy memories running through their heads as they wiped themselves up in the backs of carriages, on their way home by the light of the gas lamps.

Czarist Russia

In John T. Alexander's *Catherine the Great: Life and Legend*, the reader is repeatedly reassured that Catherine was not, in fact, involved in any kind of bestiality. Still, there's a little bit of guilt by implication going on here: what the hell is happening in your life when your biographer has to go out of his way to point out that you didn't fuck animals? The game is kind of over, at that point.

Still, Alexander sets the record straight. Catherine did not die while attempting to have sexual intercourse with a horse, which has been previously mentioned in this volume as pretty much the worst Walk of Shame situation ever devised. (Funeral Procession of Shame, I guess, but same difference.) No, no, Catherine the Great in fact died of a fit of apoplexy while sitting on the toilet. Yes, that's right. Ask yourself which is better for your reputation: dying while having sex with a horse, which is at least kind of ballsy, or being brought low by a constipation-induced stroke?

The Gilded Age

April of 1887: Susanna Medora Salter is elected the first woman mayor in the United States; Henrik Ibsen's

Rosmersholm debuts in Oslo; Anne "The Miracle Worker" Sullivan teaches Helen Keller the word "water"—and one of the key legislative landmarks in the history of the Walk of Shame is enacted, in the form of the revolutionary Voigt-Lederhorn Act. The act, signed into law by president Grover Cleveland, took a bold stand against monopolistic sexual practices, stipulating that no single person, no matter how wealthy, can send more than forty-eight percent of a locality's women on a Walk of Shame in any given thirty-day time period. The first case brought under the Voigt-Lederhorn Act was *State of Pennsylvania vs. Mortimer L. Vanderhoeg*. After several years of litigation, Vanderhoeg, a steel magnate, was forced to cut down on the number of parties thrown in his Pittsburgh mansion, and also to pay all prostitutes in real money instead of scrip.

The 1920s

The Roaring '20s saw the birth of new freedoms in sexual and personal expression for women. Suddenly, the modern woman was free of the complex belts, corsets, and bustles (fake butts) of the past. The new look, in fact, was the exact opposite of the buxom beauty standards of the Gilded Age: simple, natural, and flat as a board. This sparked something of a revolution in Walk of Shame standards. First of all, women could now walk. Second of all, in the past, the complex requirements of female presentation allowed women to hide their shame under layer upon layer of clothing—but also made the whole thing a much higher-risk endeavor, insofar as an improperly arranged bustle could create the appearance of a grotesque side-butt, or worse. Through the '20s, the chic, simple "flapper" look denied women the opportunity to fix themselves up very much, but made it a million times easier to dress oneself and flee. Just as important, the '20s saw the birth of a striking phenomenon now remembered as the "Trolley Ride of Shame."

Trolley Ride of Shame

The Great Depression

The Great Depression was a difficult time for all Americans—particularly those dependent upon subsistence agriculture for their survival. Even worse, the Depression combined with droughts and alcohol to create a disaster for many Oklahomans. As soon as the droughts began, in fact, residents of Oklahoma turned en masse to alcohol to wash away their worries, with the result that half of the state wound up sleeping with the other half and waking up feeling kind of awkward about it. So awkward, in fact, that thousands upon thousands of them fled to California, in search of a new, less-shameful start.

The Depression was a time of great privation, and those Americans who grew up during these years were left with a habit of thrift, frugality, and conservation that would last all through their lifetimes. Many men raised during the Depression, for instance, will reuse a condom up to six times before replacing it with a new one.

World War II

The period of the second World War was a time of great social and political upheaval, in addition to countless Walks of Shame, many of them crossing entire oceans and continents. Things were at their worst in the United States, where a dearth of young men and excessive condom rationing led young women to turn to more and more shameful acts in order to satisfy their physical urges. In Europe, as well, things grew sordid: the prostitution industry boomed, as it was discovered that the available supply of grateful liberated French girls *still* couldn't satisfy the rampaging sexuality of advancing Allied forces. The whole thing came to a sweaty, highly reproductive end when hundreds of thousands of soldiers returned to America and got straight to boning their ex-girlfriends. Between all of that sex and the still-running condom shortage, America saw a birth explosion that to this day threatens the survival of Social Security and Medicare.

On the plus side, the sexual practices of the average American couple took a significant turn for the exotic as the soldiers returned. It's easiest to see the reason if we look at concurrent shifts in American cuisine. Up through the 1950s, American food was completely bland, concentrating not on spice or flavor but basically on suspending food in gelatin and/or making it look like other stuff. But as these soldiers, newly exposed to the delicacies of Western Europe, returned to the States, a demand emerged for food with actual flavor—and at some point in the '50s, the Betty Crocker cookbook introduced a powerful, exotic ingredient called "garlic" into one of its pasta-sauce recipes. As things progressed in the kitchen, so did they progress in the bedroom, and countless young American girls finally allowed their husbands to touch their nipples.

The Soviet Era

Throughout the Cold War, the Soviet Union was forced to resort to greater and greater forms of propaganda and repression to keep its public organized and productive. Throughout the entire 1950s, '60s, '70s, and '80s, all Walks of Shame had to be preregistered with a specialized investigatory bureau, a process that involved standing in line for upward of four days and filling out seventeen different forms, in triplicate.

Thus, paradoxically, did the people of the Soviet Union come to reach new heights of moral rigor and familial togetherness: for the most part, men just went home and drank enough vodka to be willing to get on their immense, grumpy-looking wives.

The 1960s and 1970s

The 1960s were, as we're all told, a time of great social and political upheaval, and the spirit of the time sent shockwaves all through the world. In countries like the United States, Great Britain, and France—and in nations as distant and disparate as Brazil and Japan—young people banded together to challenge the old power structure, to fight for peace, dignity, and freedom. Then came the 1970s, and they all got distracted by hair-care products and rising gas prices, and the whole thing was largely forgotten.

Nevertheless, the spirit of the 1960s has had profound effects on our Western culture, and specifically on the Walk of Shame. Throughout the '60s and '70s, the Western world saw an increasing sexual liberation, particularly for women, who—with the increasing availability of birth control—were able to take reproductive matters into their own hands and sleep with more, and more, and more different guys. Caught up in the excitement of this "sexual revolution," people all across the country came together to hold thrilling, liberating "Marches of Shame," in which students gathered and made their way across campuses large and small, proudly proclaiming that they'd totally just gotten laid.

The 1980s

By the time 1984 came around, one word was on everyone's lips: yuppies!

Stock trading! Posh city working people drinking merlot and looking smug in terrible modern apartments filled with terrible modern art! (Also, breakdancing!)

One yuppie hallmark that everyone seemed to freak out about was the sight of working women tramping down the streets of Manhattan in business suits and blinding white tennis shoes—a whole army of them, bouncing their way to work, businesslike pumps tucked away in their awkward, unstylish gym bags. Comfort for the morning commute? Sure thing. Even better, the pre-work lobby-bathroom wardrobe change allowed career women to make their Walks of Shame *and* report for their junior-executive jobs looking bright and fresh.

Other Voices

Shame and the Career Woman: How to Have It All
by Kelly Ripa
Cohost, *Live with Regis and Kelly*

Hi. I'm Kelly Ripa, star of the excellent sitcom *Hope and Faith*. When I got a call asking me to say a few words about career women and the Walk of Shame, well—I jumped at the chance. After all, I meet women from all across the country, and they always ask me the same questions: "How can I have it all? How can I balance the hectic pace of a working woman with the pressures of being a wife and mother? Also, what the fuck is wrong with you? Are you a little insane, or just on drugs?"

Well, I may not be on drugs, and I may not know much about rock 'n' roll, but I can certainly tell you a lot about sex. Over the years—from my time in the world of soap operas to my current gig with Regis—I've struggled to find the right balance between all three elements of my life: my career, my family, and my constant, blistering urge to be gangbanged by huge groups of men.

Oh, the scrapes I've gotten into! Just last week, for instance, we were all ready to interview Peter Cincotti for *Live*. The only problem was—oops—I'd only just woken up in a New Jersey truck stop with my purse missing and my hair full of jizz. In the end, I managed to get back into the city, back to the studio, and ready to go *just* under the wire. I had to go down on three different cab drivers to get back fast enough, but you know what? Those are just the kind of sacrifices a woman has to make if she wants her makeup girl to be able to comb all the jizz out of her hair in time.

It's a constant balancing act. Another time, I'd arranged to have fourteen recently released convicts meet me in a cheap motel in New Haven, Connecticut, where they were supposed to keep me for three whole days, banging me senseless at all hours. You can imagine how excited I was. But then, just as the car service was arriving, I got a call from the studio: they needed me that weekend, they said, to do reshoots for the sitcom. And to top it all off, by the time I got off the phone with the studio, it was starting to look like little Lola was coming down with a fever. What's a gal to do? If you said "tell the studio Lola's sick, leave Lola with the nanny, and head straight out to Connecticut," good for you.

All you working women out there know how it goes: you're

torn between your career and your responsibilities as a parent, and the first things to go are your hobbies. The best advice I can give you is always to keep something in your life that's just for you—a little something to remind yourself why life is so wonderful. It's all about the simple pleasures, the me time. Take a long relaxing bath. Sit in your garden, clear your mind, and enjoy a good book. Go to your local porno theater and see how many men you can suck off before heading to work in the morning. Eat a baby. The important thing is to treat yourself well—because if you don't feel good about yourself, how successful can you be as a working woman *or* a mother?

Remember, ladies: you *can* have it all.

(Kelly Ripa was too busy to participate, so we improvised in her place.)

Dear Robin and Jay,

I live in a house with a bunch of other students. A few days ago, we brought in a keg of Icehouse, and I kind of, well, wound up doing something with one of the other girls in the house. Here's my question: is it still a Walk of Shame if you live in the same place?

—Curious in Chicago

Dear Curious,

Your question, young one, is both subtle and wise. Unfortunately, we do not believe that you have provided enough information for us to answer it. For instance, you say that you live in a "house." Are there stairs? And in the process of returning from the girl's room to your own room, did you perchance walk up or down these stairs? Did they creak? Did your other roommates rush out of their rooms to see who'd been making the bed go err-eek err-eek and find you there on the landing in only your boxer-briefs, sucking your thumb and/or cursing?

If you returned to your room by way of a hallway, how long was it? Are the rooms of any other housemates located along said hallway, between your room and that of your in-house sex partner? Did said in-house sex partner perhaps wake in a regretful mood and shove you out of her boudoir, imploring you to return to your portion of the house and never speak of this again?

Incidentally, while we assume you are a man, your handwriting is somewhat girly. Are you a girl? Was this encounter with your housemate at all lesbian in nature? If so, are there pictures, and can you send them to Jay? He is totally aware that real lesbians often have big hips and mullets, and he is totally okay with that.

Most important, how have things gone with the room-mate since this encounter? Has she spoken with you? Has there been any additional sexing? Was any of it in the butt? These are all important factors that must not be overlooked, and until such point as you can expand on them—possibly by drawing a series of explanatory pictures and diagrams—we can't really help you so much.

Sorry.

Profiles in Shame: Jay Desario

One of very few reasons I don't regret letting Jay help write this book is that it gives me the perfect excuse to talk about the most disgusting Walk of Shame I have ever personally witnessed. You see, back in college, Jay and I lived together, in a crappy split-level house near the campus of a fine, fine institution of higher learning. And one night, we had a party.

One of the attendees of said party was a girl Jay knew through some creative writing class or other, a stout, spotty, somewhat unattractive girl who wrote mediocre short stories about being Catholic. Here's the thing, though: all of these stories, as many Catholic-themed stories do, seemed to revolve around sex and guilt. Somehow, Jay got it in his head that this stout, spotty girl had some sort of flaming sexual desire that was just waiting to be tapped into—some repressed, guilty craving for sexual acts that would shock even a leather queen. And as the party wore on and Jay got drunker and drunker, he started to imagine that he was the one meant to tap into that desire.

So at party's end, Jay, being a gentleman, offered to walk this girl home. When they reached her apartment, she invited him up, and—in the words of Judge Judy—they were intimate. But oh lord was Jay wrong about the latent filth: in another great victory for Catholic guilt, she'd barely even let him under her bra.

Jay woke the next morning feeling less than well. *Significantly* less than well. In fact, his first action was to leap out of bed and race toward the door. Unfortunately, before he'd even gotten halfway there, he could feel himself about to lose it. So he looked around for anything appropriate to hurl into, and the first thing he spotted was a plastic bag from the Gap. And there you go—hork, hork, right into the bag. The bad news: when he regained his composure and looked inside the bag, he realized he'd just barfed all over three brand-new pairs of stripey socks and a pink cashmere sweater. The good news: the girl in question was still asleep. The question: What to do with the evidence?

Thus it was that Jay wound up trekking his way home

holding a plastic Gap bag full of puke. Now, you have to understand that Jay Desario is not the sharpest tool in the shed. If he had any brains whatsoever, you'd think he'd ditch the thing in the nearest wastebasket, wouldn't you? But no, not Jay. He legged his way straight home, stopping for nothing, and arrived at our hungover egg breakfast still carrying the damn thing.

The worst part of all: he actually tried to give me that sweater for my birthday.

How to . . . Remove Semen Stains

White vinegar

1. Apply vinegar to semen stains. It is a little-known fact that strong white vinegar will efficiently remove semen stains from most varieties of fabric.

2. Those of you who live in snowy northern states may also be unaware that white vinegar will effectively remove salt stains from your shoes. Salt stains, you may have noticed, are often indistinguishable from semen stains.

3. Thus, if you don't have any vinegar, and there is snow on the ground, try to convince the man in question to blow his load on your shoes and/or the hems of your jeans, whichever floats his boat.

The Walk of Shame Tourism Guide

ello, Americans: planning a vacation any-
time soon? At a time like this, with world
opinions of the United States at an
unprecedented low, it's important to be sensitive to the cultures of the places you visit. You wouldn't want to be that
typical "Ugly American" tourist, now, would you?

The first step to avoiding this stereotype is to familiarize
yourself with the customs and social practices of the nations
you'll be visiting. In no situation is this more important than
on the off chance that you find yourself taking a Walk of
Shame—which, if you're a blond college girl vacationing
anywhere along the Mediterranean, you will almost certainly
wind up doing. Below, you'll find our advice for how best to
conduct your Walk of Shame in a variety of nations. But don't
take our word for it: when in doubt, call the U.S. consulate,

and explain to them exactly where you are and what you've just done. They will totally be glad to help you.

Albania: The most important tip we can offer is a stern warning to all gay guys: just because it has thick, luxurious body hair doesn't mean it's male.

Argentina: Due to the collapse of the local currency, street crime in Argentina has increased exponentially. If you're going to sleep with someone, the best thing to do is pressure him into marrying you so you can stay in his house forever.

Australia: One of the great things about Australia is that seventy-eight percent of the men there are named Bruce. So if someone asks you what you were doing last night, just say "Bruce."

Bangladesh: Check the weather as often as possible, because the last thing you want is to be out walking when the monsoons come.

Belgium: An important thing to realize about Belgian people is that the French make fun of them for being stupid and provincial. So if your Walk of Shame isn't shameful enough, just remember this: getting with a Belgian girl is kind of the equivalent of picking up a girl from Alabama.

Brazil: Don't worry, it's a common mistake. Seriously, some of those big-ass transsexuals really, really look like women.

Brunei: Thanks to a constant flow of oil money, the Sultan of Brunei is one of the most ridiculously wealthy men in the world. His son, in turn, is rich enough to afford awesome useless shit like solid-gold toilet-roll holders and a yacht named *Tits*.[2] Ladies, if this dude wants to party with you, go for it. Totally, totally go for it.

Canada: If you're not sure how to act, how to dress, or what to say in Canada, here's a handy rule of thumb: just do whatever it was you were doing six years ago. Everyone will find you astonishingly chic.

China: Rapid industrialization in China has created a dense and exciting tangle of modern urban space, where high-tech Western opportunities exist side by side with traditional agrarian lifestyles and values. Also, ride a bike.

Colombia: A good way to get from one place to another is just to walk out in the open and wait to get kidnapped. If you want to go east, look for guerillas; if you want to go west, try paramilitary groups.

Cuba: Chances of experiencing a Walk of Shame in Cuba are, sadly, slim. Because of U.S.-led embargoes and stubborn mismanagement of the island's economy, all sex is strictly

---

[2] This is absolutely, 100% true. The attached dinghies are named *Nipple 1* and *Nipple 2*. Unfortunately, he had to sell it off after his dad got pissed and restricted him to a $300,000-a-month allowance.

rationed, and you have to stand in line for upward of six days just to cop a feel.

Czech Republic: The important thing is not to mention Kafka. Everyone finds you irritating enough already.

Egypt: No matter how much you fantasize about riding a camel under the shadow of the pyramids back from your lover's hotel, the truth is that you are probably going to get poked with a kebab stick and be paralyzed in a horrible 156-taxi pileup.

France: That woman in the picture? She is, how you say, his wife.

Germany: Before you leave the house, hostel, or apartment, make sure to check *all over* yourself and your clothes: there may be extra feces that you've somehow missed.

Great Britain: The first time someone tells you he lives in a "council estate," you may imagine an ivy-covered manor house surrounded by well-groomed green lawns. Boy, are you in for a surprise.

Greece: There's no such thing as the Walk of Shame in Greece. First of all, you'll probably be riding a Vespa. Second of all, they don't believe in shame. Seriously, just look at their swimwear.

Iceland: Oh, I know, you go to Iceland imagining all of these statuesque elf-faced fashion-model types. Then you step off the plane and remember that THESE ARE THE MOST INBRED PEOPLE ON THE FACE OF THE EARTH.

India: If you anticipate taking the Walk of Shame in India, go ahead and bring your laptop with you—you might be able to stop by the tech support center in person!

Ireland: This is one of the few places in the world where you can't get away with blaming your Walk of Shame on alcohol. Also, try not to be pregnant.

Italy: The Walk of Shame doesn't exist in Italy, mainly because everyone lives with their parents until they're thirty-eight. They just have sex on bus stop benches and then go home as usual.

Jamaica: Give yourself over to the mellow pace and friendly atmosphere of the islands! Also, don't be surprised if that "brain surgeon" you hooked up with turns out to live right down the street from you in Queens.

Japan: It's hard to have much shame in a country where you can buy panties and/or fecal porn from vending machines.

Kenya: Kenyans have long dominated world competition in the field of distance running. Some say it's the altitude; some say it's the unique build of East African runners; some say it's a cultural mind-set. No matter what the explanation, don't count on slipping out of the guy's apartment without leaving your number; he can totally catch you.

Mexico: Don't worry if you lose your identification. There are still plenty of ways back across the border, particularly if you have restaurant experience.

Netherlands: Just because prostitution is legal doesn't mean you'll feel any better about it afterward.

Nigeria: The past years have seen an ever-intensifying culture clash in Nigeria—between secular cities in the south and hard-line Islamic communities in the north, which have recently made world headlines by sentencing fornicating women to be stoned. Our advice: Walk south.

Peru: If you've slept with anyone at all during your time in Peru, please check all orifices for hidden packages of cocaine before boarding your flight home.

Poland: Forget the Walk of Shame. Here's your chance to witness the thing that President Bush kept referring to in those debates: tremble before the awesome might of the Polish military!

Russia: After just a few hours in Russia, you kind of get in the habit of having to bribe everyone to do stuff for you. But when it comes to sex, it's still prostitution, not just "part of the culture."

Saudi Arabia: Everyone worries about the lives of young Saudi women, but hey, it's not so hot for the men, either. Thanks to all that oil money, they're all expensively educated and way overqualified for the few available jobs. Plus they have very little opportunity to meet chicks. If you really want to keep America safe from terrorism, sleep with as many of them as you can: the main problem is they're just bored.

Singapore: S&M fans rejoice: in Singapore, the Walk of Shame is punishable by hot, passionate caning.

Spain: In order to understand the Spanish Walk of Shame, you need to adjust your timetable to match local schedules. You go to dinner at eleven p.m. You go back to his place at six a.m. You'll probably be the only person on the street around, say, noon.

Sweden: This is the only country in the world where you can return toys to the sex shop even after breaking the plastic. Go nuts.

Switzerland: Don't worry about taking the Walk of Shame in Switzerland. When it comes to casually walking around ignoring everything that's happening nearby, these people mastered the art back in the late 1930s.

Thailand: If you're at all tempted to have sex while in

Thailand, just wait for a busload of fat German businessmen to come by and ask them how their "tour" is going. After that, you will never want to have or think about sex ever again.

Vatican City: It's kind of hard to pull off a good Walk of Shame here, after you turn fourteen.

To Call or Not to Call

*I*t really is the question, right? The post-shame phone call is one of the touchiest points of etiquette in the entire Walk of Shame game, and we could write a whole book on this topic alone.

Now, a lot of people have a lot of theories about when you should and shouldn't call, how many days you should wait to do it, and other such things. We, however, have noticed a great big flaw in all of these theories. Call the next day, wait at least a week, blah blah blah: can you *really* hand this advice out, willy-nilly, to whoever happens to be listening? Consider your own life—if I asked you whether you wanted your hook-ups to call the next day, wouldn't you say it mostly depended on who the person was?

Therefore, we'd like to introduce another variable into the To Call or Not equation: Who is better-looking?

If you are the better-looking one of the pair, then don't call. First of all, you could probably do better. Second of all, you're just maintaining the status quo. *You're* the desirable one here, and chances are the only reason you two got together in the first place was that the other person was chasing you— buying you drinks, walking you home, complimenting your tits, etc. There's a delicate balance here, and the last thing you want to do is throw it off. Just go about your business, and if they still think you're worth putting all that work in, they'll call you.

If you are *not* the better-looking one of the pair, then you should also not call. I mean, c'mon—you don't want to embarrass yourself here. Isn't it bad enough that you followed this person around the party for like three straight hours, laughing a little too loud at all of their jokes? Have some dignity. That night on the futon you had every chance to present an argument in favor of calling you back: if it works, it works, and if it doesn't, maybe you could take some sort of class. Just don't give this person the satisfaction of calling. No matter how much you rehearse what you're going to say, you will sound totally desperate, and the *both* of you will hang up feeling even more ashamed about what happened.

"But wait," you say, "doesn't this mean that *nobody* will call *anybody*?"

Good eye, Sherlock. Nobody will call anybody, which is exactly as the world is, has been, should be, and will always be. I mean, look: if the two of you really liked each other so much, if you were really *so* interested in each other's personalities and desperately wanted to get to know each other, well . . . you wouldn't have wound up groping each other on top of a pile of Keystone Light cans, would you? No, you'd have traded numbers and made an actual date, which, if you're not aware, is what normal people do when they're genuinely interested in having any sort of relationship. Don't be ashamed about that, either. What you did was fine, and hopefully fun, and hopefully not too embarrassing—but you don't really need to speak to each other about it. Maybe, if you happen to run into each other at a party down the line, you can arrange for a repeat. But for the time being, *talking* is not where you're at.

Some of you—including overly romantic ladies and truly hard-up guys—will have trouble swallowing this rule. If you find yourself experiencing a moment of weakness, just look hard and long at the following page. Try to unfocus your eyes and see *past* the page: see, look, it's the Statue of Liberty!

DON'T CALL. DON'T CALL. DON'T CALL.
DON'T CALL. DON'T CALL. DON'T CALL. DON'T
CALL. DON'T CALL. DON'T CALL. DON'T CALL.
DON'T CALL. DON'T CALL. DON'T CALL. DON'T
CALL. DON'T CALL. DON'T CALL. DON'T CALL.
DON'T CALL. DON'T CALL. DON'T CALL. DON'T
CALL. DON'T CALL. DON'T CALL. DON'T CALL.
DON'T CALL. DON'T CALL. DON'T CALL. DON'T
CALL. DON'T CALL. DON'T CALL. DON'T CALL.
DON'T CALL. DON'T CALL. DON'T CALL. DON'T
CALL. DON'T CALL. DON'T CALL. DON'T CALL.
DON'T CALL. DON'T CALL. MAYBE JUST AS A
BOOTY CALL. DON'T CALL. DON'T CALL. DON'T
CALL. DON'T CALL. DON'T CALL. DON'T CALL.
DON'T CALL. DON'T CALL. DON'T CALL. DON'T
CALL. DON'T CALL. DON'T CALL. DON'T CALL.
DON'T CALL. DON'T CALL. DON'T CALL. DON'T
CALL. DON'T CALL. DON'T CALL. DON'T CALL.
DON'T CALL. DON'T CALL. ONLY AFTER FOUR
A.M. WHEN REALLY DRUNK AND WILLING TO DO
STUFF YOU WOULDN'T HAVE DONE LAST TIME.
DON'T CALL. DON'T CALL. DON'T CALL. DON'T
CALL. DON'T CALL. DON'T CALL. DON'T CALL.

DON'T CALL. DON'T CALL. DON'T CALL. DON'T CALL. DON'T CALL. DON'T CALL. DON'T CALL. DON'T CALL. DON'T CALL. DON'T CALL. DON'T CALL. DON'T CALL. DON'T CALL. DON'T CALL. CALL PHONE SEX LINE INSTEAD; HARDER ON YOUR CHECKBOOK, EASIER ON YOUR DIGNITY. DON'T CALL.

Dear Robin and Jay,

You two sure do seem to know a lot about the Walk of Shame. Do you have a lot of experience taking them? Also, are you two, like, together, or anything?

—Wondering in Winnipeg

Dear Wondering,

Thanks for your question. First of all, yes: we do have a lot of experience taking the Walk of Shame, some of us more than others. I (Robin) did a lot of "dating" just after college. Jay, on the other hand, was stuck in a strange and lengthy relationship with this freaky girl who played role-playing games and liked to be tied up. No one's really sure what the dynamic was there, and Jay tends not to want to talk about it.

As for whether we're together, the answer is no, and if you ever saw pictures of the two of us, you'd know exactly why. (Let's just say that one of these things is not like the other.) Before we began writing this book, though, we did decide that we'd be much more in touch with our subject matter if we took parallel Walks of Shame, just to get back into the swing of things.

To this end, we borrowed a friend's apartment, a place that was roughly halfway between our individual places of residence. We got together there, got very, very drunk, and then supposedly had sex. I don't really remember it happening, but I was pretty drunk, and Jay swears it went down, and that, furthermore, I enjoyed every minute of it. I'm not really going to argue with this, as it seems to make him feel better.

Anyway, we woke up in the morning in separate rooms—Jay's subject-changing joke is that this was because of the incredible size of his penis—and immediately set off to our respective apartments. The results?

Robin: One nasty look from old lady; two cars slowing

down, rolling down windows, then moving on; one friend who pretended not to have noticed me there (thanks, Tracy); two suggestive jokes from building manager.

Jay: Stumbled over and puked in a doorway; was given 28 cents in loose change by passing woman.

That's about the extent of our relationship: 28 cents from a passerby, and a building manager who keeps keying in whenever I'm in the shower.

How to Cope

And now we come to the heart of the matter. You've had your hook-up, and you've suffered your way through the walk home. You've faced your friends. But something still lingers, something ever so slightly wrong. And now, friends, it's time for the hardest part of all: coping with the shame.

Much as we'd like to offer a clear-cut set of rules for getting past the shame, the truth is that we're all different. Just as we all enjoy different sex acts and variously styled Walks of Shame—missionary position and a cab home; mutual masturbation and hiding behind trees; sixty-nining, getting dizzy, and winding up doing cartwheels across campus—we all must adopt different, personalized strategies to coping with the aftermath.

Here's the thing, though: we can't—and don't want to—meet you all individually for counseling. A lot of you smell kind of funny, a lot of you are *acting* kind of funny, and Jay won't even answer your mail unless you enclose a Polaroid. So after some research, we've divided the most common Walk of Shame coping mechanisms into four major categories, as follows.

Embracing the Shame

This is really the first step in the hierarchy of Walk of Shame coping, and the one part you can begin as early as on your way home. Here are some relevant facts to keep in mind:

1. Everyone is horny. This is just a fact. There is not a single person on this planet who does not have at least a limited desire for some form or other of sexual intimacy, whether it's that man in the Hyundai cruising for a $10 blowjob or that German gay-sex cannibal guy who went to jail. Also, you know your grandma? That's one lady you don't want to underestimate.

2. Not everyone can get some. Do you realize how many people are walking around just *gagging* for some action? Look around yourself: eighty percent of the people you see capped off their evenings last night with some feeble masturbation and an underdeveloped fantasy about someone or other from the WB's Friday-night lineup.

All of which leads to:

3. Be proud of yourself! You got some! If you really think everyone is judging you, you're *totally* overestimating the rest of humanity. The fact is that they're all jealous.

Try some exercises to help you to accept—and embrace—your shameful state. When you get home, stand in front of a mirror, just as you are, and stare at yourself for a full five minutes. Ask yourself: when you went out last night, why did you decide to wear this skirt? It's awfully short, isn't it? Think hard, and it will come to you that you decided to wear this skirt specifically so you could wind up, in the morning, looking exactly like this.

As you walk home, remember your mantra: I got *lucky* last night, I got *lucky* last night, I got *lucky* last night. If you repeat it often enough, maybe you'll talk yourself into it.

Working Through the Loss

A good Walk of Shame, it turns out, really *is* a form of loss. Just think of all the things that have been taken from you. Your innocence. Your underwear. Your delusional belief that you can attract the sort of man who has any idea how to please a woman. You'll never heal if you can't acknowledge that you have, indeed, been wounded.

Psychologists have devoted quite a lot of research and attention to the experience you're having, and they've organized the process into seven healthy and necessary stages.

1. Shock. This is what happens when you wake up and see the kind of person you've just let touch you. Look, your late teens and twenties are kind of a rough time: you're not sure yet what kind of person you are, and more importantly, you're not sure yet what quality of person you can manage to hook up with. You may look at the guy or girl on the other side of the bed and be shocked to learn that this is the best you can manage. You may look at the guy or girl on the other side of the bed and be shocked to realize why your friends laughed when you described this person as "cute." You may look at the guy or girl on the other side of the bed and be shocked by the kind of skin conditions that dim bar lighting can manage to conceal. Just let it happen, okay? This is a healthy part of the process.

2. Denial. This step mostly takes place between the bedroom and the front door of the building. I dunno, you think to yourself, he *was* pretty charming last night. Maybe he has a really great personality. And besides, it's not like we did all that much. I wouldn't let him have anal, would I? I'm a good girl, I can go out in public holding my head high. It's not like anyone will notice. Lots of people wear thigh-high boots and fishnets on Sunday mornings, right?

3. Anger. What the fuck does that old bitch think she's looking at? Yes, that's your anger talking. The anger stage may be a healthy one, but you should still do your best to keep it suppressed. Remember: you look like total shit this morning. It doesn't help to have you scowling at everyone.

4. Guilt. Notice that the guilt stage comes dead-center in the seven-stage process of loss. That's because it's the core of the entire matter. It's during this stage that you'll experience a moment of complete emotional clarity, especially if you're Catholic: good lord, you'll think, I'm a total slut. What have I done? And now that God has been brought into the process, you're ready for . . .

5. Bargaining. This is the most fun stage of all. A block or two from home—as you enter that zone where you really actually know people and are likely to start running into them—you'll grow desperate for some deus ex machina to rescue you. You'll make incredible appeals to a higher power, essentially promising never to have fun again if only you don't have to walk those last few steps. You'll never drink again. You'll wash your mouth out with soap. You'll stop watching porn. You'll be straight, forever and ever, if only you just don't have to do this.

6. Depression. This is the one where you realize that (a) no one is listening, (b) there is no god, (c) even if there were, she wouldn't really give a shit who you went down on, and (d) you're kind of muttering to yourself, and everyone can hear you.

7. Acceptance. Congratulations, friends: you've come out on the other side. Having exhausted every possible reaction to your loss, you key back into your home and collapse onto your bed with the feather boa still on, far too tired and pukey-looking to bother thinking about any of this for a single additional second.

Your walking-home mantra: Sprinkled Donuts Are Great; Butt Donuts Aren't. This handy mnemonic device will help you remember which stage of the loss process you should be in at any given moment. Also, it will keep you from eating butt donuts.

The Shame Vacation

After a particularly public Walk of Shame, you may be tempted to try to disappear. Sure, it sounds kind of unhealthy—we're meant to be facing our problems, right, not running away from them—but after a lot of soul-searching we've decided to endorse this method, particularly those of you who live in small towns or go to religious colleges. I mean, look: you got more than enough exposure this morning, didn't you? You deserve a break. Feel free to spend the rest of your weekend inside, watching *Buffy the Vampire Slayer* reruns and sinking into a dark pit of self-loathing.

Just make sure it's temporary. You should be able to return, on Monday, to work or class, feeling entirely yourself again. There's a line that must not be crossed. How can you tell if you've crossed it? Just look at what you're eating. You'll want to stick to a fairly normal diet, barring any hangover soft foods you're forced to resort to the day after: by Sunday you should be right back in line with a nice salad or some Chinese delivery. If you find yourself sitting in front of the television wrapped in a musty afghan, eating bag after bag of microwave popcorn and trying to convince your friends to drop off another six pints of Ben and Jerry's, things have spun out of control. Remember: if you get any fatter, your next Walk of Shame will be that much more embarrassing.

Your walking mantra should be the old Carnival Cruise Lines song, to be parroted in the shrill, irritating voice of Kathie Lee Gifford: "If they could see me now . . ."

The Laughter Method

That's why we wrote this book, after all.[3] Nothing makes you feel better about a good Walk of Shame than sitting back with your friends and laughing over the whole thing, which is exactly what you'll be doing in a few years anyway. Seriously, you will all move to different places and get different jobs and only occasionally wind up flying through one another's cities, where you'll meet up for drinks and almost immediately start reliving this experience, in front of all your *new* friends, who you'd actually fooled into respecting you as a halfway intelligent person. "Hey," your old friend will say, "remember that time you were feeling really self-conscious about your looks and tried to make yourself feel better by putting on a minidress and picking up a guy, but then you got way too drunk and when you woke up in the morning you realized the guy you were with was blind? Remember that? And then on the way home you passed out on the lawn and lay there for like two hours with your legs wide open while everyone was walking to class, until finally that one gardener came over and woke you up? Wasn't that hilarious?"

---

[3] That and the money.

If you've got friends who can get you laughing about the whole thing in the present day, you're a lucky, lucky person. If you don't, try making yourself laugh. Think of something funny. You know one thing that's funny, is farting. First of all, it makes a noise. Second of all, sometimes it *doesn't* make a noise, which is funny because everyone still notices anyway, and then they're all like, "Where did *that* come from?" Also, there's the smell.

Your walking mantra: maybe you should try farting and giggling the entire way home. Seriously, it'll be great. Everyone will think you're awesome.

In Closing

1. Clean Up

2. Feel Better

3. Good Luck